Current
CONTROVERSIES

D1090028

Politics and the Media

Other Books in the Current Controversies Series

Politics and the Media

Debra A. Miller, Book Editor

GREENHAVEN PRESS
A part of Gale, Cengage Learning

Detroit • New York • San Francisco • New Haven, Conn • Waterville, Maine • London

GALE
CENGAGE Learning·

Elizabeth Des Chenes, *Managing Editor*

© 2012 Greenhaven Press, a part of Gale, Cengage Learning

Gale and Greenhaven Press are registered trademarks used herein under license.

For more information, contact:
Greenhaven Press
27500 Drake Rd.
Farmington Hills, MI 48331-3535
Or you can visit our Internet site at gale.cengage.com

For product information and technology assistance, contact us at

Gale Customer Support, 1-800-877-4253
For permission to use material from this text or product, submit all requests online at
www.cengage.com/permissions

Further permissions questions can be emailed to permissionrequest@cengage.com

Articles in Greenhaven Press anthologies are often edited for length to meet page requirements. In addition, original titles of these works are changed to clearly present the main thesis and to explicitly indicate the author's opinion. Every effort is made to ensure that Greenhaven Press accurately reflects the original intent of the authors. Every effort has been made to trace the owners of copyrighted material.

Cover image copyright © Visions of America, LLC/Alamy.

LIBRARY OF CONGRESS CATALOGING-IN-PUBLICATION DATA

Politics and the media / Debra A. Miller, book editor.
p. cm. -- (Current controversies)
Includes bibliographical references and index.
ISBN 978-0-7377-5632-6 (hardcover) -- ISBN 978-0-7377-5633-3 (pbk.)
1. Mass media--Political aspects. 2. Social media--Political aspects. I. Miller, Debra A.
P95.8.P6455 2012
302.23--dc23

2011032688

Printed in the United States of America
2 3 4 5 6   16 15 14 13 12

FD103

Contents

Chapter 1: How Does Media Bias Influence Politics?

Chapter 2: Is the Internet Good for Democracy?

Yes: The Internet Is Good for Democracy

No: The Internet Is Not Always Good for Democracy

Chapter 3: Have Social Media Been Instrumental in Promoting Recent Revolutions?

US Secretary of State Hillary Clinton and others have argued that the new social media promote greater participation in politics and will help spread democracy and free markets, but critics point out that these technologies could have the opposite effect of encouraging polarization of politics and helping dictators to monitor and repress their citizens. Anecdotal evidence supports both views, but no one really knows which of these positions is correct because there has been little rigorous research of the issue.

Yes: Social Media Have Been Instrumental in Promoting Recent Revolutions

During the Green Movement's 2009 protests in Iran, traditional journalists left the country but Twitter became the means by which the world could watch and understand the issues and the demonstrators' hopes for greater political freedom. Without Twitter, the Iranian people would not have felt has empowered to confront the government, because Twitter provided them with the means to connect with each other and share their story with the world beyond Iran.

Chapter 4: How Will the Media's Role in Politics Evolve in Coming Years?

Foreword

By definition, controversies are "discussions of questions in which opposing opinions clash" (Webster's Twentieth Century Dictionary Unabridged). Few would deny that controversies are a pervasive part of the human condition and exist on virtually every level of human enterprise. Controversies transpire between individuals and among groups, within nations and between nations. Controversies supply the grist necessary for progress by providing challenges and challengers to the status quo. They also create atmospheres where strife and warfare can flourish. A world without controversies would be a peaceful world; but it also would be, by and large, static and prosaic.

The Series' Purpose

The purpose of the Current Controversies series is to explore many of the social, political, and economic controversies dominating the national and international scenes today. Titles selected for inclusion in the series are highly focused and specific. For example, from the larger category of criminal justice, Current Controversies deals with specific topics such as police brutality, gun control, white collar crime, and others. The debates in Current Controversies also are presented in a useful, timeless fashion. Articles and book excerpts included in each title are selected if they contribute valuable, long-range ideas to the overall debate. And wherever possible, current information is enhanced with historical documents and other relevant materials. Thus, while individual titles are current in focus, every effort is made to ensure that they will not become quickly outdated. Books in the Current Controversies series will remain important resources for librarians, teachers, and students for many years.

In addition to keeping the titles focused and specific, great care is taken in the editorial format of each book in the series. Book introductions and chapter prefaces are offered to provide background material for readers. Chapters are organized around several key questions that are answered with diverse opinions representing all points on the political spectrum. Materials in each chapter include opinions in which authors clearly disagree as well as alternative opinions in which authors may agree on a broader issue but disagree on the possible solutions. In this way, the content of each volume in Current Controversies mirrors the mosaic of opinions encountered in society. Readers will quickly realize that there are many viable answers to these complex issues. By questioning each author's conclusions, students and casual readers can begin to develop the critical thinking skills so important to evaluating opinionated material.

Current Controversies is also ideal for controlled research. Each anthology in the series is composed of primary sources taken from a wide gamut of informational categories including periodicals, newspapers, books, US and foreign government documents, and the publications of private and public organizations. Readers will find factual support for reports, debates, and research papers covering all areas of important issues. In addition, an annotated table of contents, an index, a book and periodical bibliography, and a list of organizations to contact are included in each book to expedite further research.

Perhaps more than ever before in history, people are confronted with diverse and contradictory information. During the Persian Gulf War, for example, the public was not only treated to minute-to-minute coverage of the war, it was also inundated with critiques of the coverage and countless analyses of the factors motivating US involvement. Being able to sort through the plethora of opinions accompanying today's major issues, and to draw one's own conclusions, can be a complicated and frustrating struggle. It is the editors' hope that Current Controversies will help readers with this struggle.

Introduction

> *"Media ... has evolved over the more than two centuries of American democracy as technological advancements have developed ever faster and more complex means of communications."*

Media, the plural of medium, refers to various types of communication used to transmit information within a society. From the date of America's founding, a system of free and diverse media has been viewed as vital to US democracy because it provides a way for people to express their political views and become educated about and involved in politics and government. The media also have been used historically by politicians to connect with voters and campaign for their support. The type of media available for these purposes, however, has evolved over the more than two centuries of American democracy as technological advancements have developed ever faster and more complex means of communications.

The printed word was the earliest way for people to distribute news about politics and other matters. Newspapers began as hand-written pamphlets or newsletters during the European Renaissance, and similar publications were distributed in the American colonies in the late 1600s and early 1700s. The first regularly published newspaper in America was the *Boston News-Letter*, which began in 1704. Other newspapers sprouted throughout the colonies, including the *Pennsylvania Gazette*, a newspaper founded by Benjamin Franklin in 1729. By 1775, thirty-seven newspapers existed in the American colonies, all of them small weekly papers that primarily reported political news.

These colonial publications played an essential role in the country's march toward independence. Early supporters of revolution used these first papers to push for independence from Britain and to distribute news and documents (such as the text of the Declaration of Independence) to people living throughout the colonies. Along the way, lawyers and courts developed the concept that the press should be free to report anything and criticize the government, as long as what they said was true. When the Bill of Rights was ratified in 1791, it codified this principle of freedom of the press in the First Amendment to the US Constitution, stating, "Congress shall make no law . . . abridging the freedom of speech, or of the press." As the nation matured, more and more newspapers were founded, including the well-known *New York Times* (1896) and others that developed mass readership and covered the activities of the US Congress and other political news throughout the 1900s. Newspapers have continued to be a dominant communications medium up to the present day, when more than ten thousand newspapers are published in the United States.

Radio was the next medium to develop in America. The first radio station, KDKA in Pittsburgh, began broadcasting on November 2, 1920, to announce that year's presidential election returns. Radio was an instant hit with the public, and by 1927, Americans owned more than seven million radios and the nation boasted 733 commercial radio stations, including three big radio networks—NBC, CBS, and ABC. These networks could reach millions of people with their broadcasts, a fact that brought great wealth to the broadcasters in the form of advertising dollars. Although radio became a highly popular channel for music and other forms of entertainment, it also was able to provide local, national, and world news much more quickly than weekly or even daily newspapers. During World War II, it provided the nation with breaking stories about the war and became the principal means for President Franklin D. Roosevelt to communicate with ordinary citizens—through his famous radio "fireside chats."

A new type of communications, however, soon added visual interest to radio's audio broadcasts. The birth of television, first demonstrated at the New York World's Fair in 1939 with a broadcast by President Roosevelt, may have changed US politics more than any other medium. By 1963, polls showed that TV had displaced newspapers as the main source of news for most Americans. Radio networks such as NBC, CBS, and ABC established the first television programs, paid for by advertising dollars, following the radio model.

In the years that followed, TV played a critical role in US politics. Most political experts agree that the visual contrast between John F. Kennedy and Richard M. Nixon in the 1960 presidential debates—the first to be broadcast on live television—solidified popular support for Kennedy, helping him win the election. Kennedy appeared tanned, fit, and confident while Nixon, who had recently been in the hospital, looked pale, thin, and uncomfortable in front of the camera. In addition, the Vietnam War became the first war in American history to be broadcast live, along with commentary pointing out discrepancies in government statements about the conflict. Many commentators credit this coverage as the impetus for the anti-war movement of the 1960s and 1970s. TV also was prominent, along with newspapers, in disclosing and reporting on Watergate—a political scandal involving then-president Richard Nixon that led to his resignation of the presidency in 1974.

Soon TV expanded to cable, increasing the amount of programming for viewers, and with the founding of Cable News Network (CNN) in 1980 by Ted Turner, world and national news became available twenty-four hours a day. Many commentators believe this new, 24-hour news cycle has had a significant impact on politics by allowing people to see crises and disasters as they occur around the world. In some cases, dramatic TV images have pressured US leaders to take action that they otherwise may not have considered. One example of this so-called CNN effect occurred in 1992 in Somalia. After CNN broadcast graphic pictures of starving children in the war-torn nation, then-US president George H.W. Bush sent in American Marines as part of a humanitarian mission. This mission, however, led to a 1993 battle in which Somalis brutally attacked American soldiers, killing nineteen of them and dragging one body through the streets. Largely because of this spectacle, the next president, Bill Clinton, ordered a US retreat from Somalia. Today, TV continues to provide instant cable news coverage, forcing presidents and legislators to respond quickly to events and allegations or risk being viewed as out of touch by the voting public.

Communications technology advanced again with the development of the Internet, and in recent years, the rise of social media such as Facebook and Twitter. In the 2004 presidential race, Democratic candidate John Dean's campaign was groundbreaking because it was the first to finance a presidential campaign using the Internet to solicit small donations from thousands of supporters, instead of relying on established, wealthy donors. Presidential candidate Barack Obama, in the 2008 presidential election, took the Dean campaign model a step further by using the Internet to organize supporters and communicate with potential voters without using an army of paid organizers. The creation of social media sites is the newest twist on the use of media in politics. So-called Twitter revolutions, in which social media have been used to organize anti-government protests and bring down long-time dictators, were successful in Tunisia and Egypt in 2011 and have inspired similar upririsings in many other parts of the Middle East. Many commentators are also speculating about how social media will be used in US presidential and congressional races in years to come.

The interplay between politics and the media is the subject of *Current Controversies: Politics and the Media*. Authors of viewpoints in this volume present a wide range of positions on issues such as the effect of media bias on politics, whether the Internet is good for democracy, whether social media was significant in the revolutions in Egypt and elsewhere, and how media might evolve as it continues to affect political campaigns and news coverage.

CHAPTER 1

How Does Media Bias Influence Politics?

Chapter Preface

Newspapers have been a staple of American life since the first settlers arrived in North America, tying communities together, providing important political and other information to citizens, and exposing government and business corruption for hundreds of years. Despite the advent of new technologies, such as radio and television, the printed newspaper has adapted and flourished, continuing its central role of investigating and reporting the local, national, and global news. Today, however, many newspapers—both large and small—are facing serious financial challenges that threaten their very existence, and perhaps the entire profession of print journalism.

The trouble for newspapers is declining advertising revenues. The business model for nearly all newspapers consists of selling space for commercial and classified ads, which generates the bulk of newspaper revenue. With the advent of the Internet, these advertising dollars have decreased year after year, dropping to a 25-year low in 2011, according to the Newspaper Association of America. A recent Pew Research study found that more people now get their news for free online than from a newspaper. This shift of readership from printed newspapers to online sources has enticed advertisers to follow. The classified ads, too—once a major source of income for newspapers—have gone online.

The result has been a slow but steady stream of newspaper closings around the country. This includes many long-established, big-city daily papers—like the *Rocky Mountain News* in Denver, Colorado; the *Baltimore Examiner* in Baltimore, Maryland; and the *Tucson Citizen* in Tucson, Arizona. Even the venerable *New York Times* is in financial trouble, causing it to make staff cuts, force page reductions, devote more space to advertising, and even mortgage its headquarters. Many papers have also cancelled their contracts with the Associated Press (AP)—a wire service that has provided news stories to many American daily newspapers for 137 years. AP is the world's largest news-gathering organization, with more than three thousand journalists based in one hundred countries, and it is a rich but very expensive source of articles, photographs, and other news content.

To solve this revenue problem, some newspapers have experimented with cooperatives, banding together with other newspapers to share the expenses of reporting on stories that have wide appeal. Other newspapers have tried to forge an online presence to capture the web readers that were once subscribers. Some of these newspaper websites have offered their online content for free, hoping to attract readership that can be translated into advertising dollars. Others, like the *Wall Street Journal*, charge for online access. The *New York Times*, which had provided free access to all its online readers, has recently announced a new policy of allowing readers to view up to twenty articles per month for free, but charging after that point is reached. So far, however, no one seems to have discovered the magic solution to save the newspaper industry.

The discontinuation of and cutbacks by newspapers, many commentators argue, is resulting in a loss of critical news and information for Americans. Fewer reporters means fewer stories will get covered, and shrinking pages means fewer stories get published. At the same time, the expense of paying for news stories from news agencies like the Associated Press is causing some local newspapers to drop these services altogether—another loss of important news for some regions. And in some communities, local newspapers have closed completely, leaving residents with no source of local or regional news. In-depth investigative journalism work may even fall by the wayside, threatening newspapers' traditional role as watchdog for the public.

A reduction of real news, some people say, will have dire effects on democracy. Citizens will be less informed and no one will know what the real truth is on many important public issues. Already, the strong trend is towards opinion journalism—news that is either subtly or openly biased toward either conservative or liberal political views. Unlike traditional news sources, such as newspapers and network TV programs, cable news broadcasters like Fox News and MSNBC flaunt their political leanings and attack politicians who disagree with them. A wealth of Internet news sites, too, tend to offer biased news analysis and commentary rather than original investigative news stories. Gone is the effort to be as objective as possible, long associated with professional journalism. On the other hand, many commentators have pointed out that traditional news sources themselves have often shown another type of bias—a pro-establishment, pro-corporate tendency due to the fact that many news sources are large corporate conglomerates with close ties to the government. The viewpoints in this chapter address this issue of media bias and how it is affecting politics and government.

A Liberal Media Bias Demonizes Conservative Values

William F. Jasper

William F. Jasper is senior editor for the New American, *a bi-weekly magazine whose editorial policy supports limited government, protection of the US Constitution and the freedoms it guarantees, and individual responsibility.*

On February 12 [2010], Dr. Amy Bishop, an associate professor of neurobiology at the University of Alabama in Huntsville, pulled out a pistol during a staff meeting and opened fire on her fellow faculty members, killing three and wounding three others. Chances are you heard or read about the case. And you may have read or heard in some of the follow-up reporting about other bizarre incidents earlier in her life, such as her 1986 "accidental" shooting of her brother and her being a suspect in the 1993 case of a pipe bomb that had been mailed to a Harvard professor with whom she had had a dispute. But, most likely, you didn't read or hear that the 44-year-old, Harvard-educated Bishop was a fanatical "Obama Girl."

According to the *Boston Herald*: "A family source said Bishop . . . was a far-left political extremist who was 'obsessed' with President Obama to the point of being off-putting." Now, you can be fairly certain that if Professor Bishop had been a Ron Paul [a Libertarian congressman] supporter, or a "right-winger" of any type, we would be hearing still about how the dangerous "ideology of hate" had driven her to her excesses. Dr. Paul would be hounded relentlessly by reporters demanding to know if he assumes any responsibility for the hate that caused these murders, and if he felt the need to alter his stand in favor of individual rights and the Second Amendment. . . .

Another Example of Liberal Bias

The case of Joseph Stack is similarly instructive. On February 18, the computer software developer intentionally crashed his private airplane into an office complex in Austin, Texas, killing himself and an office manager for the Internal Revenue Service. Thirteen others were injured. Stack's suicide note—a rambling rant against the IRS, corporations, and the supposed injustices he had endured—was immediately seized upon by politicos on the Left and their allies in the media to proclaim Stack a poster boy for the burgeoning Tea Party movement. The title for a February 23 op-ed by Robert Wright in the *New York Times'* online "Opinionator" column was "The First Tea-Party Terrorist?" In that column, Wright says: "In the end, the core unifying theme of the Tea Partiers is populist rage, and this is the core theme in Stack's ramblings." Wright, moreover, claims that the psychological "ingredients" that propelled Stack on his suicide/murder mission—"a conspiratorial bent, a deep and personal sense of oppression, an attendant resentful rage—can be found in the movement, if mainly on its fringes. There are some excitable Tea Partiers out there."

According to Lydia Khalil, a resident fellow at the Council on Foreign Relations, and one of the organization's supposed terrorism experts, Stack's suicide attack shows "it's time to stop putting the serious and growing threat of homegrown right-wing extremism—and the acts of violence it sometimes provokes—on the relative back burner." Khalil's March 11 op-ed in the *New York Daily News*, entitled "Stop Minimizing the Right-wing Terror," predictably quotes a Southern Poverty Law Center (SPLC) report, which ominously claims that "right-wing militias, ideologically driven tax defiers and sovereign citizens are appearing in large numbers around the country."

Jonathan Capehart, in a February 18 *Washington Post* op-ed, wrote that "after reading [Stack's] 34-paragraph screed, I am struck by how his alienation is similar to that we're hearing from the extreme elements of the Tea Party movement."

New York Magazine's Chris Rozvar wrote: "In fact, a lot of his rhetoric could have been taken directly from a handwritten sign at a tea party rally." The *Daily Kos*, a blog popular with the left-leaning, warned that the Stack murder/suicide "should inject a bit of caution into the anti-government flamethrowers on the right."

The mainstream media seem terminally afflicted with a compulsion to issue daily baseless warnings on the dangers of "right-wing extremism" . . . yet they don't have the time (or inclination) to cover the stories of left-wing violence.

Much of the mainstream media news and commentary was only slightly less inflammatory than this April 18 headline from the left-wing blog, OuterPartyPress: "Right-Wing Terrorist Crashes Plane into IRS Building. Teabagger Hate Bears Fruit."

Of course, it turns out that Joe Stack was no "right-winger" at all, and had no connection to any Tea Party group. From what can be pieced together from his rantings, he could be more accurately described as a left-winger, a textbook example of Marxist "alienation." He rages against capitalism, banks, insurance companies, drug companies, Wall Street, President [George W.] Bush, the Catholic Church . . . and yes, the IRS. Stack ends his long-winded suicide note with this apparent paean to Karl Marx, author of the *Communist Manifesto*:

The communist creed: From each according to his ability, to each according to his need.

The capitalist creed: From each according to his gullibility, to each according to his greed.

Amy Bishop and Joseph Stack are not isolated cases. The teleprompter readers and hack writers of the mainstream media seem terminally afflicted with a compulsion to issue daily baseless warnings on the dangers of "right-wing extremism" and to regurgitate every breathless announcement from the professional fundraisers and propagandists at the SPLC—yet they don't have the time (or inclination) to cover the stories of left-wing violence. The following are but a few examples of many that fell through the cracks while the Big Media was stirring the hate pot against the Right:

- Norman Leboon of Philadelphia was arrested March 27 for issuing death threats against Rep. Eric Cantor (R-Va.) and his family. Leboon, who contributed $505 to Barack Obama's presidential campaign in 2008, posted threatening videos on YouTube aimed at Cantor, the second-ranking Republican in the House and the only Republican Jewish member of Congress. Leboon's profanity-laced video told Cantor: "You are a liar, you're a pig . . . you're an abomination. You receive my bullets in your office, remember they will be placed in your heads. You and your children are Lucifer's abominations."

- The previous week Rep. Cantor's campaign office in Richmond, Virginia, was struck by a bullet. The same media that lavished huge coverage on alleged death threats against several Democratic Congressmen gave short shrift or no coverage to the Cantor stories.

- Several thugs wearing SEIU (Service Employees International Union) T-shirts attacked Kenneth Gladney, a black conservative, at an August 6, 2009 Town Hall meeting with Rep. Russ Carnahan (D-Mo.) in St. Louis. The SEIU goons were caught on tape as they brutally beat, punched, knocked down, and kicked Gladney, who had simply been peacefully handing out the historic "Don't Tread on Me" flags. One of the attackers called Gladney a "son of a n****r." Gladney, who sustained significant injuries in the unprovoked attack, is pursuing civil action against the three attackers who were arrested and are also being prosecuted on criminal battery charges. The attackers were part of a large SEIU pro-Carnahan contingent at the Town Hall, and the SEIU has been one of President Obama's staunchest supporters. The SPLC, NAACP [National Association for the Advancement of Colored People], Congressional Black Caucus, NBC, and *New York Times* have not rushed to report Gladney's case or to demand accountability from Carnahan, Obama, or the SEIU.

- Lloyd Marcus is a singer who has performed at 34 Tea Party rallies in 16 states, oftentimes singing the National Anthem. Lloyd Marcus happens to be black. But since his presence contradicts the mainstream media meme which holds that the Tea Parties are a racist, whites-only movement, he is often cropped out of "news" broadcasts and photographs. He has also experienced vicious racial verbal attacks, but *not* from the Tea Partiers. "The racial hate expressed against me all came from the left, people who support President Obama's radical socialist agenda," says Marcus on his blog. "Unfortunately, my deleted email box is littered with numerous messages expressing the following: 'You are the dumbest self hating f****** n***** I have ever seen!'"

- Radio talk-show host and former CNN newsman Lou Dobbs was subjected to a nationwide hate campaign aimed at driving him off the air, primarily because of his outspoken opposition to amnesty for illegal aliens and his support for increased border security. He and his wife were also subjected to many death threats and in October 2009 were shot at, with a bullet striking their home. The hate campaign, which portrayed Dobbs as a racist and terrorist, was organized by Drop-Dobbs.com, a coalition of left-wing groups that included the National Council of La Raza, Media Matters, the National Hispanic Media Coalition, the Southern Poverty Law Center, Voto Latino, and the Labor Council for Latin American Advancement. "Lou Dobbs is a terrorist. He is encouraging the American people to hate Latinos," said Fabian Arias, a pastor of the Sion Lutheran Church in East Harlem and an activist in the DropDobbs campaign.

To the above-cited incidents could be added literally hundreds of others in which leftist agitators from MoveOn.org, Code Pink, A.N.S.W.E.R., ActUp, NARAL, LaRaza, Greenpeace, Earth First, SEIU, AFLCIO, and other groups have physically attacked and injured peaceful protesters or police officers, started riots, and endangered public safety. However, based on the coverage in the "mainstream" media it would seem that the only threat to civil discourse, and the only threat of hate and violence, emanates from the political Right.

Orwell and Goldstein

Some time in high school or college most of us read *Nineteen Eighty-Four*, George Orwell's grim novel of a dystopian future under the iron-fisted rule of The Party and Big Brother. One of the most chilling features of existence in Orwell's foreboding creation is the Two Minutes' Hate, daily sessions in which Party members must demonstrate their loyalty by watching a film depicting The Party's enemies, and whipping themselves into a frenzy of hatred against the enemies and love for Big Brother. The chief enemy in these daily brainwashing films is Emmanuel Goldstein, whose face morphs onto the screen after vicious enemy soldiers with hideous facial expressions charge the viewers with guns blazing. The fictional Goldstein serves The Party's needs as the designated "enemy of the state," providing an object against which citizens can rant and vent their ire, rather than directing their rage against the regime that is oppressing them.

> *Anyone who resides even slightly to the right of the political-correctness fault line . . . [is] likely to get smeared as being anti-government, anti-Semitic, racist, extremist, seditious, violent, paranoid—and of course, hateful.*

In America today, it seems, the Two Minutes' Hate sessions have found a number of stand-ins for Goldstein: Tea Party activists, global-warming "deniers," Obama-Care opponents, constitutionalists, pro-life activists, opponents of homosexuality, Second Amendment advocates, states' rights proponents, foes of amnesty for illegal aliens, home-schoolers, and Christians who adhere to orthodox biblical teaching and traditional values.

In short, anyone who resides even slightly to the right of the political-correctness fault line established by Barack Obama, Nancy Pelosi, and the avatars of Big Government/Big Media/Big Hollywood/Big Academia is liable to be targeted for the Goldstein treatment. What that means, in real terms, is that if one falls into any of the above-mentioned categories, or happens to be what is usually described as a political/economic/social "conservative," you are likely to get smeared as being anti-government, anti-Semitic, racist, extremist, seditious, violent, paranoid—and of course, hateful.

In an April 9, 2010 online piece for *Newsweek* entitled "A Surge of Hate," Evan Thomas and Eve Conant warn that "antigovernment extremists are on the rise—and on the march." In the printed magazine version of the four-page article, which is dated April 19, the word "HATE" is emblazoned in huge letters covering half a page. The *Newsweek* duo then begin their article by targeting Stewart Rhodes and Oath Keepers:

Stewart Rhodes does not seem like an extremist. He is a graduate of Yale Law School and a former U.S. Army paratrooper and congressional staffer. He is not at all secretive. . . . Rhodes says he has 6,000 dues-paying members, active and retired police and military, who promise never to take orders to disarm U.S. citizens or herd them into concentration camps. Rhodes told a *NEWSWEEK* reporter, "We're not a militia." Oath Keepers do not run around the woods on the weekend shooting weapons or threatening the violent overthrow of the government. Their oath is to uphold the Constitution and defend the American people from dictatorship.

But by conjuring up the specter of revolution—or counter-revolution—is Rhodes adding to the threat of real violence? Oath Keepers are "a particularly worrisome example of the 'patriot' revival," according to Mark Potok of the Southern Poverty Law Center (SPLC), which monitors hate speech and extremist organizations.

Newsweek *authors smear the millions of peaceful, law-abiding Americans who are legitimately concerned over the complete breakdown of our border security.*

Newsweek's Thomas and Conant admit that Rhodes "does not *seem* like an extremist"—and they present no evidence to indicate that he *is* "an extremist," whatever that may mean to them. Yet they proceed to indict him as such by implication and innuendo, solely on the basis of a claim by an SPLC spokesman that Oath Keepers are "particularly worrisome." Why are they so "worrisome"? SPLC's Potok cites no crimes committed, no threats, no violent or racist rhetoric, no advocacy of illegal or immoral acts. Perhaps someone will dig up some statement or action by Rhodes or one of his Oath Keeper members to justify concern—but unless and until they do, is it not the height of indecency to attempt to conflate Oath

Keepers with Oklahoma City bomber Timothy McVeigh, as Thomas and Conant try to do?

In similar fashion, the *Newsweek* authors smear the millions of peaceful, law-abiding Americans who are legitimately concerned over the complete breakdown of our border security, by likening them to Klansmen carrying out lynchings. They write: "Fear of 'the other' has long fueled hate crimes, from the torture and lynchings by the Ku Klux Klan beginning in the late 1800s, to the violence of the 1950s and '60s, to the virulent anti-immigrant groups today."

According to *Newsweek*, "The current surge of fear and loathing toward Obama" is based on race. It quotes Columbia University historian Alan Brinkley as saying, "There's a big dose of race behind the real crazies." And, he says, it is "scary."

The major media first tried to kill the Tea Party movement by ignoring it, but when that didn't work they turned to the familiar smear tactic.

The Obama camp—those in the political sphere and in the media—have, of course, hurled the charge of racism to intimidate, silence, and marginalize all critics, going back to his presidential campaign and continuing to the present. Over the past few months the race card has been used with a vengeance in an attempt to beat down the Tea Party movement.

Attacking the Tea Party

Brent Bozell of the Media Research Center reports that the major media first tried to kill the Tea Party movement by ignoring it, but when that didn't work they turned to the familiar smear tactic. Bozell says his group "found only 19 news stories on the Tea Party movement for the entire year [of 2009] on ABC, CBS and NBC. The Obama family dog received more attention." Bozell puts the coverage in context:

How anemic is this? Compare those 19 stories in all of 2009 with 41 stories the networks gave the "Million Mom March" against gun rights in 2000—and all before the math-challenged protest even happened. Consider racist and anti-Semitic Rev. Louis Farrakhan's "Million Man March." On Oct. 16, 1995, ABC, CBS and NBC together aired 21 stories just on one night.

The difference in tone was just as dramatic. Amazingly, the Tea Parties were assumed to be racist, but Farrakhan's event was not. ABC anchor Peter Jennings devoted all but 75 seconds of his newscast to promotional goo for the Nation of Islam.

Bozell then compares that to the Tea Party stories. "The victory of Sen. Scott Brown in Massachusetts spurred heavier network TV attention, another 42 stories in 2010." "But," he notes, "now that they had to cover the Tea Party, the tone turned negative: Overall, 27 of 61 stories (44 percent) openly suggested the movement was fringy or extremist." Bozell continues:

Contrast ABC's Peter Jennings then with ABC's Dan Harris now. Farrakhan was somehow a uniter, not a divider. But Harris warned Tea Party protesters "waved signs likening Obama to Hitler and the devil. . . . Some prominent Obama supporters are now saying that it paints a picture of an opposition driven, in part, by a refusal to accept a black president."

And with that, everyone associated with the Tea Party movement, and everyone in sympathy with the Tea Party movement, had just been neatly tarred with the racism brush. What dramatic selectivity of "news judgment"! At left-wing rallies, reporters consistently and easily ignored hateful and extremist podium speeches from protest organizers. They paid no attention to objectionable signs. "Bush Lied, Thousands Died!" Big deal!

But at a conservative event, they go searching high and low for the kookiest, fringiest protester in a crowd of tens of thousands, so they can smear the entire crowd as a racist gathering.

Following the ObamaCare vote on Saturday, March 20, tens of thousands of protesters gathered peacefully at the Capitol in Washington, D.C., to register their opposition to the legislation. That is when several members of the Black Congressional Caucus staged a "race card" stunt to change the dynamics of the debate. Led by Rep. John Lewis (D-Ga.), the Black Caucus contingent traipsed through the Tea Party throng and then claimed that they had been subjected to racial taunts by a group chanting the "N-word." Immediately *that* became the big story and headlines about racism in the Tea Party movement and the racist opposition to ObamaCare were re-circulated. House Minority Leader John Boehner decried the incident as "deplorable" and other Republican leaders also were forced to switch focus from debating the real issues of healthcare to denouncing the racial incident.

Now, if the event had happened as the Congressional Black Caucus (CBC) claims, it would have been an unfortunate incident, but no fair-minded person would lambaste tens of thousands of otherwise innocent demonstrators for the actions of a few who clearly did not represent the whole. But there is good reason to suspect that the incident never even happened, and that the entire affair is a vicious lie concocted by the CBC to discredit Obama-Care opponents and the Tea Party movement. The best reason is that, so far, the CBC has not produced one independent witness or a single audio or video recording to substantiate their serious charge.

A Conservative Media Bias Tilts Government Policies to the Right

E.J. Dionne Jr.

E.J. Dionne Jr. is an op-ed columnist for the Washington Post *who writes on national policy and politics, and who has served as a political commentator for a number of news organizations.*

A media environment that tilts to the right is obscuring what President Obama stands for and closing off political options that should be part of the public discussion.

Yes, you read that correctly: If you doubt that there is a conservative inclination in the media, consider which arguments you hear regularly and which you don't. When Rush Limbaugh sneezes or Newt Gingrich tweets, their views ricochet from the Internet to cable television and into the traditional media. It is remarkable how successful they are in setting what passes for the news agenda.

The power of the Limbaugh-Gingrich axis means that Obama is regularly cast as somewhere on the far left end of a truncated political spectrum. He's the guy who nominates a "racist" to the Supreme Court (though Gingrich retreated from the word yesterday), wants to weaken America's defenses against terrorism and is proposing a massive government takeover of the private economy. Steve Forbes, writing for his magazine, recently went so far as to compare Obama's economic policies to those of Juan Peron's Argentina.

Democrats are complicit in building up Gingrich and Limbaugh as the main spokesmen for the Republican Party, since Obama polls so much better than either of them. But the media play an independent role by regularly treating far-right views as mainstream positions and by largely ignoring critiques of Obama that come from elected officials on the left.

This was brought home at this week's annual conference of the Campaign for America's Future, a progressive group that supports Obama but worries about how close his economic advisers are to Wall Street, how long our troops will have to stay in Afghanistan and how much he will be willing to compromise to secure health-care reform.

When Rush Limbaugh sneezes or Newt Gingrich tweets, their views ricochet from the Internet to cable television and into the traditional media.

In other words, they see Obama not as the parody created by the far right but as he actually is: a politician with progressive values but moderate instincts who has hewed to the middle of the road in dealing with the economic crisis, health care, Guantanamo and the war in Afghanistan.

While the right wing's rants get wall-to-wall airtime, you almost never hear from the sort of progressive members of Congress who were on an America's Future panel on Tuesday. Reps. Jared Polis of Colorado, Donna Edwards of Maryland and Raul Grijalva of Arizona all said warm things about the president—they are Democrats, after all—but also took issue with some of his policies.

All three, for example, are passionately opposed to his military approach to Afghanistan and want a serious debate over the implications of Obama's strategy. "If we don't ask these questions now," said Edwards, "we'll ask these questions 10 years from now—I guarantee it."

Polis spoke of how Lyndon Johnson's extraordinary progressive legacy "will always be overshadowed by Vietnam" and said that progressives who were challenging the administration's foreign policy were simply trying to "protect and enhance President Obama's legacy by preventing Afghanistan and Iraq from becoming another Vietnam."

As it happens, I am closer than the progressive trio is to Obama's view on Afghanistan. But why are their voices muffled when they raise legitimate concerns, while Limbaugh's rants get amplified? Isn't Afghanistan a more important issue to debate than a single comment by Judge Sonia Sotomayor about the relative wisdom of Latinas?

Polis, Edwards and Grijalva also noted that proposals for a Canadian-style single-payer health-care system, which they support, have fallen off the political radar. Polis urged his activist audience to accept that reality for now and focus its energy on making sure that a government insurance option, known in policy circles as the "public plan," is part of the menu of choices offered by a reformed health-care system.

There is a deep and largely unconscious conservative bias in the media's discussion of policy . . . [that] cuts off more vigorous progressive perspectives.

But Edwards noted that if the public plan, already a compromise from single-payer, is defined as the left's position in the health-care debate, the entire discussion gets skewed to the right. This makes it far more likely that any public option included in a final bill will be a pale version of the original idea.

Her point has broader application. For all the talk of a media love affair with Obama, there is a deep and largely unconscious conservative bias in the media's discussion of policy. The range of acceptable opinion runs from the moderate left to the far right and cuts off more vigorous progressive perspectives.

Democrats love to think that Limbaugh and Gingrich are weakening the conservative side. But guess what? By dragging the media to the right, Rush and Newt are winning.

There Are Many Types of Media Bias

Dbug

Dbug is the online name for an anonymous writer who frequently blogs at Daily Kos, *an American political blog that publishes news and opinions from a progressive point of view.*

Here are some thoughts I've had about media bias. I use the word "media" as a plural. When I refer to a "medium," I mean a TV show, radio show, a newspaper, a magazine, a website, etc. . . .

Types of Media Bias

I probably missed a few, but I've come up with several different types of media bias.

Political Bias is when a medium (or a reporter) consistently favors a certain political party or issue or political point of view. *Fox News* is right-wing; *Mother Jones* is left-wing. Rachel Maddow is left-wing; George Will is right-wing. Sometimes you'll see bias about a specific issue. The *Seattle Times* was founded over 100 years ago and it's been transferred down to the fourth (or fifth?) generation. At least once a year, they print an editorial about the evil unfairness of the inheritance tax, because that's one tax that affects the owners.

Advertising Bias is when a medium either praises its advertisers or avoids criticizing them. The most egregious examples of this are the free newspapers that print an ad for a restaurant right next to a highly favorable review.

Corporate Bias is when a medium avoids reporting bad news about their corporate owners or their subsidiaries. One example of many: Both *Fox News* and the *Wall Street Journal* are owned by Rupert Murdoch. If Murdoch defends something said by Glenn Beck, is Murdoch giving his honest opinion or trying to protect his bottom line?

Label Bias is when certain code words are used for individuals or groups of people. A great example comes from wars. What's the difference between terrorists, rebels, revolutionaries, Marxists, and freedom fighters? "Tribes" is another good code word—it usually means dark-skinned people (in Somalia or Rwanda or Pakistan, say). When the Northern Ireland troubles were ongoing, nobody ever talked about Catholic tribes and Protestant tribes. When Afghans were fighting against the USSR [the Soviet Union], they were mujahedeen. Now they're fighting against us and they're Taliban. Another label that bugs me is "inner-city" (which usually means African American). I could provide a zillion examples of label bias.

Herd Mentality Bias—which might be called inside-the-beltway reporting or just plain laziness—is when reporters and media talk about an issue for one reason: Other reporters and media are talking about it. So, let's say Barack Obama bows when he meets the Japanese Emperor. In my opinion, it's no big deal. Then Rush [Limbaugh] says something nasty about Obama. And George Will writes about it. Rachel Maddow invites someone on her show. And Jon Stewart shows the video. Fox News claims that Obama embarrassed all Americans. And Maureen Dowd writes a column. Ten people write Daily Kos diaries about it. For God's fracking sake, just because everyone's talking about it doesn't mean it's worth talking about.

Have you ever seen six-year-old kids playing soccer? They all run to the ball and there are 20 kids poking their shoes at it. At some point, the ball pops out and they all run over the new location. That's the herd mentality.

Internet Bias is a form of gullibility. I can't understand how people believe "if it's on the internet, it must be true."

You can find truthers, birthers, freepers, anthropogenic climate change deniers, protocols of the elders of zion, ufo people, bigfoot people, Mormons-are-going-to-hell people, crazy yogurt diets, the-world-will-end-in-2012 people, new world order masonic bilderberg tri-lateral conspiracy theorists, and so on. And that's not even counting stuff like READ THIS IMPORTANT EMAIL AND FORWARD IT TO ALL YOUR FREINDS.... If it's all caps and it's misspelled, it must be true!

The Unbiased Bias is when a reporter feels compelled to report both sides of a story. Yes, the Earth is spherical and it rotates on its axis and it revolves around the sun. You don't need to mention the theory that Atlas is holding up the earth and standing on a turtle. The sun is not Apollo's chariot. Atomic bombs do not contain evil demons. 99% of climate researchers agree that temperatures are going up (the other 1% are either idiots or paid shills). Jesus did not ride on dinosaurs. I know you're trying to be fair and balanced, but at some point, you shouldn't include a second opinion that makes no sense whatsoever.

Other Biases: I probably missed a few categories of bias. I don't doubt I'll be schooled.

Is Being Biased an Unethical or Bad Thing?

I would argue that it's not so bad. I like Rachel and Keith [Olbermann], knowing that both of them are fairly liberal, and they're both pretty smart. When I watch them, I know I'm probably going to agree with them. I don't watch Beck or [Bill] O'Reilly, because they're idiots.

Some people say that news media should report just the facts and be unbiased. But that's impossible.

Let's say some man kills his wife and two kids and commits suicide. Maybe he lost his job and belonged to a church that said the man is superior to the woman and should provide for his family. Should that be reported?

Or let's say an airplane crashes in Africa. The plane was made by the Russians and the airline wasn't very good about maintenance. And the owner of the airline was a cousin of the president of the country. Should that be reported?

At some point, people who hear or read the news want to know more about the details. Reporters need to dig into the motivations and, at some point, they have to explain how something happened. It's Hutus versus Tutsis. It's Sunnis (who believe one thing) versus Shiites (who believe something else). The Pakistani Supreme Court overruled the President and lawyers marched in the streets. Jean Marie Le Pen is not just a conservative politician. He's a racist . . . who hates immigrants and gays and abortions.

It's not possible to report in an unbiased way about Health Care Reform. Obama says one thing, [John] Boehner says something else. [Nancy] Pelosi gets quoted. [John] McCain says something totally idiotic. Reporters should be unbiased, in a general way, but they should interpret and explain as well.

Some people say that news media should report just the facts and be unbiased. But that's impossible.

Two Stories from My Life

About ten or fifteen years ago I worked with a guy who was a Republican. He was a decent person and he was very good at his job. But if we talked about politics, he would get angry and accuse me of being brainwashed by the liberal media. We eventually decided we shouldn't talk politics with each other. Which was fine with me.

Around the same time, I met a stranger in a bar. We started talking and he told me that the media are all right-wing tools of the evil corporate overlords and they don't report on the important issues. "Give me one example of an important issue not reported on," I said. "East Timor," he said. "So how do you know about East Timor?" I asked. He named a couple of magazines and mentioned a book by Noam Chomsky. "But those are media, which means the media are reporting on that issue," I said. He said that he was talking about mainstream media (MSM), like *Time* magazine or CNN or the local newspaper. I asked, "Do you read *Time* or watch CNN?" He said no he didn't, because they're right wing.

> *Right-wingers often believe that the MSM [mainstream media] have a liberal bias, whereas left-wingers often believe the MSM have a conservative bias. . . . Maybe they're both right.*

Right-wingers often believe that the MSM [mainstream media] have a liberal bias, whereas left-wingers often believe the MSM have a conservative bias. They can't both be right, or can they? Maybe they're both right.

Hostile Media Bias

I saved the best part for last. Are the media actually biased? Or do we just perceive the media as biased? Here's . . . an abstract for a study conducted in 1985—25 years ago. And it's an I/P topic. Please, please, please, don't start a flame war about Israel and Palestine. This diary is about media bias.

> After viewing identical samples of major network television coverage of the Beirut massacre, both pro-Israeli and pro-Arab partisans rated these programs, and those responsible for them, as being biased against their side. This hostile media phenomenon appears to involve the operation of two separate mechanisms. First, partisans evaluated the fairness of the media's sample of facts and arguments differently: in light of their own divergent views about the objective merits of each side's case and their corresponding views about the nature of unbiased coverage. Second, partisans reported different perceptions and recollections about the program con-

tent itself; that is, each group reported more negative references to their side than positive ones, and each predicted that the coverage would sway nonpartisans in a hostile direction. Within both partisan groups, furthermore, greater knowledge of the crisis was associated with stronger perceptions of media bias. Charges of media bias, we concluded, may reflect more than self-serving attempts to secure preferential treatment. They may result from the operation of basic cognitive and perceptual mechanisms, mechanisms that should prove relevant to perceptions of fairness or objectivity in a wide range of mediation and negotiation contexts.

So, the pro-Israel people thought the media had a bias against Israel. And the pro-Arab people thought there was a bias against Arabs. Both groups thought the media were biased against them. People notice the media bias against their beliefs more than they notice the bias in favor of their beliefs. Which explains why left-wing people think the media have a conservative bias. And right-wingers think the media are a bunch of liberals.

And here's a quote from *Wikipedia*'s piece about Hostile media effect:

This effect is interesting to psychologists because it appears to be a reversal of the otherwise pervasive effects of confirmation bias: in this area, people seem to pay more attention to information that contradicts rather than supports their pre-existing views. This is an example of disconfirmation bias.

Studies have found hostile media effects related to other political conflicts, such as strife in Bosnia and in U.S. presidential elections.

An oft-cited forerunner to Vallone's et al. study was conducted by Albert Hartorf and Hadley Cantril in 1954. Princeton and Dartmouth students were shown a filmstrip of a controversial Princeton-Dartmouth football game. Asked to count the number of infractions committed by both sides, students at both universities "saw" many more infractions committed by the opposing side, in addition to making very different generalizations about the game in general. Hartorf and Cantril concluded that "there is no such 'thing' as a 'game' existing 'out there' in its own right which people merely 'observe.' . . . For the 'thing' simply is not the same for different people whether the 'thing' is a football game, a presidential candidate, Communism, or spinach."

People notice the media bias against their beliefs more than they notice the bias in favor of their beliefs.

I thought it was worth writing a diary about. And it might start a conversation.

Yes, in some ways the media are biased. But, also, if you have a political (or college football or I/P) bias of your own, you will think that the media are biased against you.

A Highly Polarized Media Contributes to Government Dysfunction

Ethan Zuckerman

Ethan Zuckerman is a researcher at the Berkman Center for Internet and Society, a research center at Harvard University that focuses on cyberspace issues.

A recent [April 2011] *New York Times* poll suggests that Americans are in a dark mood. 70% of people think the country is moving in the wrong direction, a number not seen since the peak of the Great Recession two years ago. Their frustration may stem from higher gas prices or continued unemployment, but at least some commentators believe that a key factor is popular frustration with a dysfunctional government that doesn't seem able to address the issues the US is facing.

The near-shutdown of the US government a few weeks back helps illustrate the dysfunction. Web pioneer Philip Greenspun tries to put the fight over $38 billion in spending in perspective by dividing budget numbers by 100 million. With a little mathematical analogizing, the nation's $3.82 trillion federal budget and $1.65 trillion debt turns into a family income of $21,700, annual spending of $38,200 and credit card debt increasing by $16,500 annually. At this scale, the debate over "the largest domestic spending cut in US history" turns into a spat over a $380 cable bill when, perhaps, we should be worrying about defaulting on the mortgage.

Polarized Discourse

Fareed Zakaria, often one of the more thoughtful commentators on America's role in the world, offers little encouragement in a recent essay in *Time*. Titled "Are America's Best Days Behind Us", Zakaria warns that the US is starting to look a bit like Britain after World War II, suffering from a sclerosis tied to success. Content with our position in the world, he warns, we may have lost sight of the fact that other nations are investing more heavily in infrastructure, education and research and development, and that our comfortable economic leadership may be rapidly receding into the past. He observes that the US government is spending $4 on the elderly (who vote) for every $1 spent on those under 18 (who don't), and wonders whether we've moved from attempting to win the future to protecting the past, a stance that's likely to be futile in the long run.

Our political discourse has become highly polarized . . . to a degree that makes many of us uncomfortable and unwilling to engage in debates with those we disagree with.

Zakaria pins the blame squarely on our political culture, specifically on an allergy to compromise that apparently affects both Republicans and Democrats. Solutions to America's problems involve raising taxes and cutting benefits, making government more efficient and investing in future-oriented programs, building infrastructure and sponsoring research and development. Our political discourse has become highly polarized, perhaps not to an unprecedented level, but to a degree that makes many of us uncomfortable and unwilling to engage in debates with those we disagree with. Attempts to discuss improving the tone of politics in the wake of the shooting of Arizona congresswoman Gabrielle Giffords foundered, in part, because they were deemed to be partisan. Accused (unfairly, I think) of having provoked the shooting by placing a crosshairs over Giffords district in her campaign literature (an unwise and unkind, if unfortunately common, political tactic), Sarah Palin declared that criticism of her political incivility was a "blood libel". . . a term so emotionally charged for many Jewish Americans that she helped further polarize political debate. We can't talk about polarization because that conversation is, you guessed it, highly polarized.

Conflicting Boundaries

Brooke Gladstone, co-host of the indispensable radio show On the Media, introduced her listeners to a useful set of ideas for understanding why polarization makes political discourse so difficult. Trying to tackle the question, "Does NPR have a liberal bias?", she invoked media theorist Daniel Hallin. In 1986, Hallin introduced the idea that we can understand journalistic ideas in terms of three "spheres", widely recognized, though rarely articulated. The "sphere of consensus" includes ideas that are so widely agreed upon that they are generally uncontroversial. As Brooke puts it, "Democracy is good, slavery is bad, all men are created equal. Here truths are self-evident and journalists don't feel the need to be objective." Then there's the "sphere of legitimate controversy", issues we are used to arguing over, like taxation policy, abortion, gun control and capital punishment, where reasonable people can disagree, and where journalists generally focus their attention. Finally, there's the "sphere of deviance", where ideas are deemed unworthy of a hearing. Brooke offers the "pro-pedophilia" position as an example of the deviant sphere, but we might term a discussion that questioned the wisdom of democracy or the fairness of capitalism as deviant within most American media discourse.

The issue we face in a highly polarized media environment is that we're no longer in agreement on the boundaries of these spheres. Hallin, interviewed by Gladstone, notes that when he offered the three sphere model, he believed there was a single set of spheres journalists agreed upon. The argument was about whether the boundaries of the spheres were set in the right places, or whether they limited legitimate debate.

Now we face multiple, conflicting sets of spheres. In one, the question of whether President Obama was born in the United States is within the sphere of legitimate controversy; in another, that question is in the sphere of deviance. Those who see the question as deviant are offended that the press would legitimate these ideas by giving them attention and coverage; those who see the question as a legitimate controversy are upset it receives so little attention and coverage. It's hard to discuss a question of bias when observers are using sufficiently different definitions of consensus, deviance and controversy. NPR's coverage may be primarily focused on the sphere of legitimate consensus for some fraction of listeners, and well into the sphere of deviance for others.

The issue we face in a highly polarized media environment is that we're no longer in agreement on the boundaries of . . . spheres [of consensus, legitimate controversy, and deviance].

It's worth noting that one tactic for social change involves working to shift these spheres. Perhaps to embrace the radical notions we need consider to escape Zakaria's sclerosis, we need to shift the boundaries of the sphere of legitimate controversy and entertain notions that might have been revolutionary and deviant. But the divergence of spheres into two or more conflicting sets can make political debate frustrating. When we argue about Obama's citizenship, one side presents what they perceive to be the relevant facts, while the other is frustrated the debate is even taking place.

Using Values, Not Facts

I work with a number of progressive organizations that seek change in the US and around the world on topics like media reform, human rights, alternatives to incarceration and improved education. Faced with misinformation about issues they care about, either through poor reporting or the distortions of political opponents, most organizations conclude that what's needed is more facts. The solution might be better reporting, impartial factchecking or the naming and shaming of those who knowingly spread falsehoods. While I strongly support the first two, I don't think facts will fix the problems we face from polarization.

A 2008 study by the Pew Research Center for People and the Press found that a belief that global warming was caused by human activity was closely correlated to political affiliation: 58% of Democrats believed human activity was causing global warming while only 27% of Republicans did. Democrats with more education were more likely to connect climate change to human activity—75% of Democrats with college degrees see a connection, while only 52% of Democrats with less education do. The opposite is true with Republicans—the Pew report states, "Only 19% of Republican college graduates say that there is solid evidence that the earth is warming and it is caused by human activity, while 31% of Republicans with less education say the same."

Faced with misinformation about issues they care about . . . most [progressive] organizations conclude that what's needed is more facts.

In general, more education—and, presumably, a better set of intellectual tools to seek out facts—correlates to a stronger belief in human factors leading to climate change. But once we separate survey respondents by ideology, the picture is more complicated. More education—more facts, perhaps—leads to polarization, not to persuasion. (I found this finding very helpful in understanding one of the most fascinating and baffling stories I've recently heard on [the NPR program] This

American Life. Wondering whether exposure to scientific research, carefully explained, could change the mind of a climate change skeptic, Ira Glass arranged a radio conversation between Dr. Roberta Johnson, the Executive Director of the National Earth Science Teachers Association, and a very smart teenage Glenn Beck fan. At the end of twenty minutes of what sounded to me like very persuasive arguments, the young woman explained that she wasn't convinced—she wanted to hear both sides of the controversy, not the "argument" the earth science teacher was offering.)

A truly excellent article by Chris Mooney titled "The Science of Why We Don't Believe in Science" offers some hope for deciphering this conundrum. Offering a tour of research in neuroscience and cognitive science, Mooney makes the case that our reasoning is heavily rooted in emotion and in our values. Phenomena like confirmation bias (a tendency to overweight information that agrees with our preconceptions) and discontinuation bias (the tendency to discount information we disagree with) contribute to a pattern of "motivated reasoning", where our emotions distort and shape our "rational" thinking. Mooney suggests that there's deep neurological reasons for this behavior—we literally have a hair-trigger "fight or flight" reaction to types of information that challenge our belief systems.

As a result, confronting a highly polarized argument with facts frequently backfires. Presented with more information, Democrats find more reasons to support a conclusion that climate change has human causes, while Republicans find reasons to believe the opposite.

While Mooney's analysis offers deep links into the scientific literature to understand the dimensions and implications of motivated reasoning, he doesn't offer much detail for the activist seeking to persuade an opponent, or a citizen simply hoping for more civil, reasoned debate. But the closing words of his article offer a possible path forward: "You don't lead with the facts in order to convince. You lead with the values—so as to give the facts a fighting chance."

It's possible to read this advice from Mooney as an invitation to pick up a well-thumbed copy of George Lakoff's "Don't Think of an Elephant." Lakoff is right to point out that Republicans have often been better than Democrats at presenting their ideas in a way that appeals to moral frames. But his works focus so heavily on the language used rather than the underlying values that it's easy to oversimplify his idea to a game of choosing the right words to persuade a different audience. When progressive activists try to go down this path, they study the language of right-wing punditry and conclude that we need our own media, including blowhard radio hosts and a left-wing Fox News. This strategy hasn't worked very well—these outlets don't mobilize the progressive base, nor do they convince opponents.

Leading with values to give the facts a chance requires more than sprinkling business-friendly or family values fairy dust on progressive policies.

Taking the challenge Mooney presents of leading with values to give the facts a chance requires more than sprinkling business-friendly or family values fairy dust on progressive policies in the hopes that they'll suddenly appear palatable. It requires the much harder work of understanding the values a conservative voter brings to the table and finding common ground between our issues and their values. It may mean seeking common ground on energy policy by exploring the ways in which wind turbines help farmers in the mountain West create an alternative revenue stream for their ranches, or seeking a reexamination of mandatory drug sentences laws based on a desire to cut state spending by trimming prison budgets.

Richard Cizik's vision of "creation care", a vision of environmentalism rooted in scriptural interpretation is more than a frame designed to persuade Evangelical Christians to take green issues seriously. Creation care isn't "spin" created by a progressive thinktank designed to broaden the green movement's base. It's the result of the long, complex process of an influential Evangelical thinker wrestling with the factual evidence that suggests a human role in climate change and biblical injunctions to humans to act as stewards of God's creation. And because Reverend Cizik is deeply rooted in the evangelical community, he's able to find common ground, shared values and, eventually, new language that a secular environmentalist would have trouble utilizing in a way that didn't ring false.

Viewing the World Differently

If the path that leads from polarization towards common ground is rooted in understanding values as well as facts, we've got a challenge—how do we start listening to the needs, wants and aspirations of people who view the world differently?

I think David Simon, the creator of the remarkable TV drama The Wire may have an answer. In an interview with Bill Moyers, he talks about the frustration he felt as a reporter with the *Baltimore Sun*, trying to get readers—and fellow newspaper writers—to understand how damaging the "war on drugs" was to their city. "And I would think, 'Man, it's just such an uphill struggle to do this with facts.' When you tell a story with characters, people jump out of their seats, and part of that's the delivery system of television."

The power of The Wire, a series with Dickensian intricacy and an emotional punch that makes it both hard to watch and hard to stop watching, doesn't come from seeing ourselves in the characters on the screen. I'm as committed to the notion of a universal recognition of humanity as the next progressive, but that's not what makes Omar Little, the gay stick-up man who only robs drug dealers so unforgettable. He's a rich, textured character, carefully crafted, with aspirations, dreams and values which we likely don't share, but which Simon allows us to understand. Simon's story helps us understand that many people believe that the US is creating a new caste system through a failed war on drugs . . . and that they may have a point. . . .

Is America on the wrong track? Are things getting better or worse? Has our political culture become so toxic that compromise is no longer possible? These aren't questions we can answer through marshaling collections of facts. They're questions that force us to tell stories about our values, to listen to the stories our fellow citizens are telling, and to seek the elusive common ground that allows us to have a functional society.

The Media Bias During the 2008 Presidential Election Favored Winners

Tony Rogers

Tony Rogers is a reporter, author, editor, and journalism profes-
sor who writes about journalism and the media on About.com,
an educational website.

The press likes a winner.

That's the conclusion of the latest Pew Research Center study on news coverage of the [2008 presidential] election.

The study, which tracked campaign news for the six weeks following the conventions through the final debate, found that coverage of Sen. John McCain was "heavily unfavorable."

"Unfavorable stories about [Republican presidential candidate John] McCain outweighed favorable ones by a factor of more than three to one—the most unfavorable of all four candidates," the study said.

That's the line that's sure to raise the hackles of the right-wing-talk-radio-Fox-News punditocracy, and probably rightly so.

But what the study really reveals is that the press likes whomever is leading in the polls, and prefers horse-race political coverage to examinations of policy.

Study Highlights

Coverage of McCain started out positive but turned negative when he reacted to the Wall Street meltdown, and grew more negative still when he began attacking Sen. Barack Obama's character.

Coverage of Obama started negatively after the conventions, but turned more positive as he moved up in the polls. The most positive stories about him centered on tactics.

Coverage of Gov. Sarah Palin started positively but turned sour in the wake of her bungled interviews and news about her public record. Still, she received more positive coverage than McCain, and got roughly triple the coverage of Sen. Joe Biden.

Biden "was nearly the invisible man," the study says. Aside from the veep debate, he received little coverage, most of it negative (even more negative than Palin).

Rising poll numbers seem to trump any liberal bias the media might have.

Essentially, the study says, the candidate who was winning got the most favorable coverage. That, of course, raises the chicken-or-the-egg question of which came first—slightly more favorable of Obama, or his surge in the polls.

But rising poll numbers seem to trump any liberal bias the media might have. A similar Pew study in 2000 found that George [W.] Bush got more positive coverage than Al Gore.

Perhaps the most damning finding is that 53 percent of coverage was horse-race reporting about strategy and polling, compared to just 20 percent on policy. Maybe it's no wonder that so many voters say they still don't know where the candidates stand on major issues.

Enterprise reporting, where journalists dug up original stories about the candidates instead of simply echoing what was said on the campaign trail, was scarce, and may become scarcer still with widespread layoffs in the news business, the study found.

CURRENT
CONTROVERSIES

CHAPTER 2

Is the Internet Good for Democracy?

Chapter Preface

President Barack Obama's 2008 presidential campaign made history because of its innovative use of the Internet—both to raise money and to organize supporters. Many commentators have credited the campaign's use of new media such as Facebook, YouTube, and Twitter for winning the presidency for Obama. President Obama, however, merely took advantage of the technology available to him and built on the technological successes of previous campaigns. The Obama campaign showed that the Internet has truly revolutionized the way political candidates wage their campaigns.

One innovation of the Obama campaign was its use of social networks to raise millions of dollars from hundreds of thousands of small donors. In the past, politicians for national office have traditionally sought donations from CEOs and lobbyists—people whose business and political connections allow them to bundle thousands of small donations from friends, employees, and acquaintances to create large contributions of $100,000–$200,000 or more. George W. Bush, for example, used this method to set fundraising records in the 2000 presidential campaign. The Obama fundraisers, however, were approximately nine thousand ordinary people who volunteered to solicit their friends and family by hosting fundraising web pages for Obama. This Internet-based system allowed fundraising emails to go viral, as each person forwarded fund requests to his or her circle of family and friends. Using this system, Obama raised a record-breaking total of $600 million in campaign contributions from more than three million people—many of them online donations of amounts under $100.

The Obama campaign also used the Internet to connect with and organize supporters in a way that previously would have required an army of volunteers and paid organizers on the ground. For example, it placed videos on YouTube that could be distributed online and traded between friends—a technique that provided Obama with free advertising. According to Obama campaign manager Joe Trippi, the YouTube videos were watched for 14.5 million hours—advertising that would have cost $47 million if it had been purchased on TV. Candidate Obama also used the Internet to respond to political attacks in depth. In response to criticisms about Mr. Obama's relationship with a controversial preacher, the Reverend Jeremiah Wright, Obama gave a long, thoughtful speech about race that was watched by more than 6.7 million people. Obama online supporters also created more than thirty-five thousand voter groups based on geographical or other ties, and organized hundreds of thousands of events during the course of the race, including a thousand phone banks during the last week of the campaign. The campaign effectively employed other new technology as well, such as phone texting. One notable text sent by the campaign, for example, announced that Obama had selected Joe Biden to be his running mate. These technology tools helped Obama, a relative newcomer to politics, win 52 percent of the vote.

But President Obama's success with Internet fundraising and organizing is just the latest example of how the Internet is changing politics. This process began in the late 1990s when political groups such as the progressive MoveOn and the conservative FreeRepublic set up websites to influence voter opinion. Around the same time, political bloggers began to proliferate online. In 1998, Minnesota gubernatorial candidate Jesse Ventura became the first politician to use the Internet for distributing information to voters, such as major campaign announcements, positions on key issues, and fundraising requests. Shortly thereafter, the 2000 presidential election saw the Bush campaign use email lists to organize supporters and both sides benefited from Internet ads. Perhaps the biggest breakthrough, however, came in 2003, when Democratic presidential candidate Howard Dean utilized an online tool, Meetup, to help supporters organize and raise money. By the fall of 2003, Dean supporters had set up eight hundred monthly meetings in support of Dean's campaign, and Dean often found himself mobbed at campaign appearances. Meetup also provided the Dean campaign with a list of email addresses, which it used to raise millions of dollars from thousands of small donors. In one year, by using these Internet tools, Dean's campaign grew from an underfunded outsider to one that broke the Democratic record for fundraising in a presidential campaign. Howard Dean ultimately did not win his party's nomination, but he helped to revolutionize Democratic fundraising. By 2006, politicians from throughout the political spectrum had embraced Dean's Internet formula for both fundraising and advertising. Libertarian presidential candidate Ron Paul, for example, raised $6 million in twenty-four hours on December 16, 2007, from online donations—the biggest one-day fundraiser ever.

It was Barack Obama's innovation, however, to make use of the new social media Internet sites. After his election, President Obama continued to use the Internet while governing; his administration set up numerous websites to keep in touch with supporters and explain new governmental programs to constituents. In the future, political experts predict that the Internet will play an even more important role in political campaigns and governments around the world, but commentators disagree about whether this will ultimately be a positive trend. The authors of the viewpoints in this chapter provide a range of views on a key question—whether the Internet is good for democracy.

The Internet Helps Build Democracies

Barrett Sheridan

Barrett Sheridan is a staff writer who covers business and technology for Newsweek, *a weekly US news magazine.*

There aren't many ideas that unite former U.S. president George W. Bush and his successor, Barack Obama. But one safe topic for conversation would be Internet freedom and the power of technology to foment democratic revolutions. In mid-April [2010] Bush welcomed to his new think tank in Texas six dissidents who used Web tools to oppose dictatorships, applauding them as examples "of how the Internet can be effectively used to advance the freedom agenda." Obama, meanwhile, has made Internet freedom a centerpiece of his foreign policy, and in a speech in Beijing [China] late last year [2009] hailed "access to information" as a "universal right."

The Internet and Revolution

This kind of talk taps into a wide vein of techno-utopianism that has been around since at least the dawn of the Web. The Internet is disruptive by nature, rapidly overturning business models and mores, so it was natural for tech-savvy foreign-policy thinkers to believe that dictatorships, too, would fall with the click of a mouse. That, of course, didn't happen. In fact, quite the opposite is true, say a growing number of cyberskeptics. Autocrats have "mastered the use of cyberspace for propaganda," says Evgeny Morozov, one of the smartest and best-known cyberskeptics. Worse, they've learned to mine online information, such as Facebook profiles, for intelligence purposes. "The KGB used to torture to get ahold of this data," says Morozov. "Now it's all available online." In short, say the cyberskeptics, the Internet will lead to the entrenchment of dictatorship, not its end.

But that is a shortsighted view, and one predicated on the trend line over the last few years, in which autocracies appear to have gained the upper hand against democrats. If it seems as if they have, it's because the hardliners are playing catch-up—they've finally recognized the existential threat posed by the Internet. The color revolutions in former Soviet republics, the post-election protests in Iran, the saffron revolt in Burma, and smaller-scale Chinese demonstrations against pollution and corruption—all prominently featured the use of online tools and mobile phones to organize protesters and project their message around the world.

[The Internet] is biased toward open, decentralized systems, i.e., democracies.

The cyberskeptics are right that this is not a one-sided fight; Iran's Basij militiamen can use Facebook, too. But the Internet represents "the largest increase in expressive capability in human history," as the writer Clay Shirky puts it, and because of its open, decentralized architecture, it is biased toward open, decentralized systems, i.e., democracies. For instance, the use of Twitter by protesting youths in Moldova last year to create a flash mob in the capital city of Chisinau illustrated just how powerful an organizing and communicating tool the Internet is, even when limits are placed on it. And when dictators fight back against it, they're pushing against a wall of water. "It's a cat-and-mouse game," says Daniel Calingaert, the deputy director of programs at Freedom House— each new government restriction is met with an inventive workaround, which prompts new restrictions. In Moldova the government blocked cell-phone reception in the square where protesters had gathered. So the protesters simply walked a couple of blocks away to post tweets, then returned to the square. Their tweets dominated the micromessaging service for days.

Trumping the Despots

Of course, there is a logical end to any cyber cat-and-mouse game that goes on long enough. During Burma's saffron rebellion in 2007, the junta maintained its heavy-handed Web censorship tactics, blocking many foreign sites and e-mail programs, but protesters easily circumvented them and managed to post photos and firsthand accounts of the regime's brutality, including a video of a soldier shooting a Japanese reporter dead. On Sept. 29 the junta decided it had had enough, and simply shut down the country's two Internet service providers. To the techno-utopians, this was a splash of ice-cold water to the face, suggesting that the government in power virtually always holds the trump card. But in one way the junta's extreme reaction actually revealed the futility of its censorship. Their choice was a binary one: accept that the Web cannot be controlled, or eliminate it altogether. Choosing the latter sets a nation on a path to becoming the next Hermit Kingdom, a decision that almost every nation is unwilling to make.

The cyberskeptics also forget that the path toward democracy is a long one, and that the Internet is, in many places, less than 10 years old. The late political scientist Samuel Huntington once remarked that the wisest democratic reformers "tend to be leery of simple solutions and of revolutions." Massive protests and toppled statues make for great TV, but most of the hard work comes well before and lasts long after the putsch. It's during that long process—which academics such as Huntington call "democratic consolidation"—that the Web's impact will be most felt. Mobile banking and e-commerce are helping more people join the ranks of the middle class, typically the first group to agitate for freedoms. Bloggers and tweeters are fulfilling the watchdog role in places where the mainstream media is muzzled. Election monitoring can now be performed by anyone, thanks to open-source platforms like Ushahidi, which facilitate anonymous reporting. In other words, Presidents Bush and Obama are right to agree on this issue: the digital masses trump the despots.

The Internet Is Making Big Money TV Ads Obsolete

Mary Kate Cary

Mary Kate Cary is a political and business speech writer who previously served as the White House speech writer for President George H.W. Bush.

The outrage was immediate: The Supreme Court decision that struck down restrictions on the use of corporate funds in political advertising, *Citizens United v. Federal Election Commission*, is "devastating to the public interest" (President [Barack] Obama) and a "disastrous rollback" of campaign finance laws (MoveOn.Org) and promises a "windfall" (*New York Times*) of big-money television ad buys by groups like the U.S. Chamber of Commerce and the AFL-CIO.

The Rise of New Media

But really, does anyone think that in 2020—or maybe even 2015—we'll still have big money television ad buys, regardless of who's paying for them? The magnitude of technological change over the past 10 years has been astonishing; the next 10 will surely be more so. I'm not saying that there won't be televised political ads at all anymore or that corporations won't find new and creative ways to spend their money. But the collective outrage focused on a top-down, big-money view of politics, well, that's so ... last century. If the goal of television ads is to motivate viewers to vote, volunteer, or give money, there are far better ways to reach people, thanks to the new media.

New social media are already changing the way organizations attract supporters. The American Red Cross raised a record $8 million plus for Haitian relief efforts via Twitter, which, according to the Nielsen Co., has become the top source of discussion about the quake, followed by online video and blogs. The potential mobile universe of grass-roots text messagers is now over 136 million—an emerging market and communications network for nonprofits, small businesses, and political campaigns.

If the goal of television ads is to motivate viewers to vote, volunteer, or give money, there are far better ways to reach people, thanks to the new media.

Most Americans have a cellphone and access to a computer these days, and many of us have moved to a much more digital existence. We've gained hundreds of cable TV channels and satellite radio stations, millions of bloggers, and literally billions of Web pages. The media today are more diffuse and chaotic than ever.

A New Communications Paradigm

The result is a new paradigm in political communications, and both parties are using it. Very little of it has to do with expensive political advertising on mass media. Look at your desktop, and you'll see the ways the new media are changing the political scene from the bottom up:

- *News you can choose*: Dan Pfeiffer, the White House communications director, recently told the *New Yorker* magazine, "With the Internet, with YouTube, with TiVo, with cable TV, people are selective viewers now. . . . People approach their news consumption the way they approach their iPod: You download the songs you like and listen to them when you want to listen to them." That affects the way reporters spend their days and the way campaigns craft their message.

- *Share this*: Sharing is emerging as a way of distributing the news—tweets from the streets of Iran and from the rubble of Haiti have been retweeted hundreds of times in a new, virtual form of word of mouth. The White House's Facebook page has nearly half a million fans; its Twitter feed has 1.7 million followers. That's no surprise: President Obama was the first candidate to announce his White House run via Web video and his vice presidential pick by text message. Don't forget that Sarah Palin began the whole "death panels" discussion not by giving an interview but by posting the idea on her Facebook page, which then got shared with thousands of friends.

- *Like it*: By clicking on a "thumbs up" or "thumbs down" icon, constituents can give politicians an instant read on opinions and positions posted on their Web pages, sort of a rudimentary straw poll that is faster, cheaper—but less accurate—than a high-priced telephone poll.

- *Connect with others*: During the height of demonstrations in Iran, street organizers tweeted safe locations for impromptu protests—building "flash mobs"—to great effect. Similarly, last-minute organizational details for tea parties, town hall meetings, and even State of the Union-watching events get posted on Facebook pages and tweeted to supporters. It sure beats passing out fliers at subway stops, as political organizers used to do.

- *Donate now*: John McCain first harnessed the Internet for fundraising after his 2000 New Hampshire primary victory; by 2007, Ron Paul raised $4 million online in one day, despite being largely ignored by the media. Barack Obama raised hundreds of millions online over the course of his presidential run, and in just the last two weeks of the senatorial race in Massachusetts, Scott

Brown raised $12 million from 157,000 donors, according to online consultants Mindy Finn and Patrick Ruffini, who helped Brown. Most politicians would rather have thousands of individual givers than a few big corporate donors, and the Internet makes that much easier.

[There is] a new paradigm in political communications, and both parties are using it. Very little of it has to do with expensive political advertising on mass media.

Politicians have long sought to go around the mainstream press filter—from fireside chats, to whistlestop tours, to snail-mail newsletters—but the new media take it a step further by even more directly connecting them with voters. And the technology is moving quickly. Last fall, a Conservative Talking Points iPhone app came out; a few days ago the White House unveiled its new iPhone app, with live-streaming video of presidential events. Who knows what's next?

The Internet "has reorganized the way Americans do everything—including elect their leaders. Candidates who would have had no chance before the Internet can now overcome huge odds, with the people they energize serving as the backbone of their campaign," Finn and Ruffini wrote in the *Washington Post*. To me, it's a good thing that the new media give a bottom-up boost to candidates facing overwhelming odds. And that far outweighs the supposedly devastating effect of a few big corporate donors buying top-down television ads.

Internet Activist Alliances Could Challenge Both Right and Left Corporate Insiders

Jane Hamsher

Jane Hamsher is an author, political commentator, and writer whose work has appeared in numerous political publications. She also is the founder of FireDogLake.com, a progressive website that features news articles and an online community.

I appreciate the opportunity to speak on today's topic: "Can the internet fix politics?" . . . Whether the internet can "fix" politics . . . depend[s] on what you think is wrong with politics. And as someone who has spent the past several years working in online activism, I would say that the problems in our political system are monumental and spin out from what I call the Cycle of Decay.

Not to be overly melodramatic, but at the moment, it's becoming more and more apparent that corporate America and political elites of both parties are locked in an embrace that threatens to scuttle the world economy, the environment and our system of representative democracy.

And we don't even have a language to talk about it. We measure every political debate along a right-left axis, with rhetoric left over from the culture wars of the 90s. But in doing so, we're firing past the true villains—the Masters of the Universe who skillfully manipulate tribal prejudices to insure that it is their interests, and not those of the public, that are the ones always being served.

Jane Hamsher, "Can the Internet Fix Politics?," FDLaction, June 3, 2010. fdlaction.fire doglake.com. Copyright © 2010 by fdlaction.firedoglake.com. All rights reserved. Reproduced by permission.

Crony Capitalism

So how does this system work? Well, it starts with crony capitalism—defined as "an economy in which success in business depends on close relationships between businesspeople and government officials."

And are they ever close. During the past decade the most hotly contested political battle in Washington DC has not been over gay rights or abortion or taxes or the war—it's been the battle for PhRMA's [the pharmaceutical industry] money.

When George [W.] Bush was in the White House Congress passed Medicare Part D, with the caveat that the government couldn't negotiate for pharmaceutical prices. Now how does a Congress obsessed with "fiscal responsibility" pass a law forcing the government to pay whatever price an industry wants to charge them?

And yet, they did.

So when the Democrats took back Congress in 2006, they made a big show of passing drug price negotiation, championed by Nancy Pelosi, Rahm Emanuel and Barack Obama. But since George Bush would never sign it, there was no danger of it actually passing.

Corporate America and political elites ... are locked in an embrace that threatens to scuttle the world economy, the environment and our system of representative democracy.

And when Barack Obama could sign it, the Democrats cut a deal with the pharmaceutical companies that guaranteed there would be no prescription drug price negotiations—in exchange for the low low price of $150 million in political advertising.

At the time, my blog FDL was engaged in an online campaign to provide competition and control health care costs by passing the public option—something that 80% of the country, the President and a majority in both houses said they supported. But as I watched the debate on the Senate floor with my colleague Jon Walker, we shook our heads in dismay and realized the problem was much bigger than we'd ever imagined. It was clear that there was nobody on either side of the aisle who was willing to tell the truth and speak up for the people they were elected to represent, and that overwhelming popular support is not a factor in passing legislation.

The public never heard about the true struggle that drove the health care debate because the national media and the political dialog is incapable of much above the level of demagoguery. And in the end, the blogs that had been powerful independent voices during the Bush era became largely subsumed by partisan dynamics.

Other Examples of Corruption

But the deal that drove $300 billion into PhRMA's coffers is not an isolated example. They are the rule, not the exception. And what do companies do when they know their profits are thus guaranteed?

That their markets are protected from competition?

Companies become incentified by our political system to take risks—risks with terrible consequences.

That no matter what kind of a mess they make, they can just take those profits and plow a small fraction of them back into the political system, and lay their losses off on the taxpayers?

They take excessive risk, knowing they will never have to pick up the tab if things go wrong.

It inevitably leads to disaster.

The damages from the BP oil spill could easily go into the tens or even hundreds of billions of dollars. Yet top BP executives felt free to take big gambles with safety and the environment because Congress had capped the liability of the oil companies at $75 million. There was no downside.

And so these companies become incentified by our political system to take risks—risks with terrible consequences.

In 2008, the excessive risk-taking of Wall Street banks brought the entire world economy to the verge of collapse or so we were told. Congress moved with bipartisan swiftness unseen since the Terry Schaivo crisis to approve emergency bailout funds.

If I leave you with one thought today, I hope it is this: in 2009, the Center for Responsive Politics reported that banks who received TARP funds spent $77 million on lobbying and $37 million on federal campaign contributions.

Their return on investment was 258,449 percent.

We are rewarding failure with the funds they use to further bribe and contort our political system. We are pouring concrete into our problems. Small businesses may be building better mousetraps, but they can't bring them to market because the megacorps are gaming the system. The companies that could drive economic growth and create jobs are stifled as the incentive for competition and innovation is extinguished.

That is a problem that cannot be solved on either the right or the left alone, because both the Democrats and the Republicans play critical roles in perpetuating it.

During the health care debate, Republicans demagogued "socialism" to kill competition in form of the public option that the insurance companies didn't want. Then it was left to the Democrats to pass the insurance mandate to guarantee their market, strip out language that would make them subject to anti-trust laws, and guarantee profits by prohibiting prescription drug price negotiation or reimportation.

Likewise, the banks weren't crazy about paying into a fund that would absorb some of the costs should they find themselves in trouble again. And it came straight out when the GOP started screaming about it. But the banks wanted to make sure that if they DID get into trouble that the taxpayers would be there for them, so once again the Democrats were left to bat cleanup.

So basically, after screwing everything up royally, the banks were allowed to write the very legislation that was supposed to safeguard the system and rein them in.

Why do people allow their representatives to do these things? How is it that they return them to office again and again even in the face of this open criminality?

One word: Tribalism.

If you won't vote for several billion dollars in no-bid contracts for Halliburton to overcharge for monogrammed towels for soldiers in Iraq who don't have sufficient body armor, you don't support the troops. If you don't support forcing Americans to pay 8% of their income to the insurance companies they hate, you obviously want Sarah Palin to be President. If you don't support the agenda of your "tribe," as determined by corporate money pouring through the coffers of validators in your respective interest groups, you're a homophobe. Or a moonbat. A bigot or a teabagger. A baby killer, a godless socialist, an ignorant redneck or a tree-hugging hippie freak.

The online world has been able to force some accountability by challenging party authority on both sides.

Now all of those things might well be true. But it rarely has anything to do with the outcome, which is almost always the same: Halliburton (or Chevron or Pfizer or Monsanto) gets what they want because to oppose the ability of the party leadership to rob you blind means the other side might win, and nothing could be worse than that.

Online Populists

The online world has been able to force some accountability by challenging party authority on both sides, carving out notable populist victories that have toppled corporatist politicians who voted for the bank bailout.

And I have to say that of late, the right has done a better job of it than we on the left have, and they're scaring the daylights out of the Republican party.

Politics online is largely siloed on opposite sides of the right-left cultural divide, [allowing] ... party operatives [to frame] the debate around advancing corporate interests.

But we're doing our best to catch up.

Online populists on both the left and the right are vilified in the media for bucking party authority and for supporting "extremists," as if those politicians who dub themselves "centrists" are anything other than radical corporate lackeys whose actions would have been considered criminal in another era.

But it's unclear whether anyone elected to replace them will be immune from the institutional pressures that lead to exactly the same pattern of behavior. Without serious systemic change, it is unlikely.

Politics online is largely siloed on opposite sides of the right-left cultural divide, and as such our websites easily flooded by party operatives who frame the terms of the debate around advancing corporate interests. Thus we frequently redouble the limitations of the status quo rather than acting as an independent political force.

We did have one notable political success recently, in a hard fought battle to audit the federal reserve. Did you know that Congress can not audit the federal reserve? That [investment company] JP Morgan's Jamie Dimon is on the board of the Fed [the Federal Reserve, the nation's central bank], and he gets to know what goes on with the institution that prints our money, but the Chairman of the Senate Banking Committee can't? A lot of people don't know that.

The bill to audit the fed was championed by Republican Ron Paul and Democrat Alan Grayson.

We worked hard to whip support from libertarian and progressive leaders on both sides of the aisle. [Conservative lawyer] Bruce Fein and [taxpayer advocate] Grover Norquist made cause with [labor leader] Richard Trumka and [liberal economist] James Galbraith. [Conservative groups like] Freedomworks, the National Taxpayers Union and the John Birch Society joined with [progressive organizations such as] the Campaign for America's Future, US PIRG and Public Citizen. Conservative blog Red State, liberal blog Firedoglake and finance blogs like Zero Hedge and Naked Capitalism wrote about the subject diligently and raised the issue onto the radar of both parties.

We caught them in a pincer move.

And despite the fact that both the Fed and the Treasury lobbied against it, and Republican Senator Judd Gregg threatened to filibuster it as "dangerous populism," in the end it passed: 96-0.

> *By making peer-to-peer connections . . . , the structure of the internet could potentially facilitate [an] . . . alliance of outsiders capable of taking on insiders on discrete issues.*

Five votes cast against it switched when they saw which way things were going. In the end, despite the furious well-funded lobbying of the banks, everyone in both parties was afraid to vote against it. The Republicans were terrified of what had just happened to Bob Bennett [a senator who lost in a Republican primary election due to Tea Party activism], which cut off the ability of our "centrists" to triangulate against the left and find refuge in "principled conservatism." They all just looked like hacks for the banks.

It won't work in every instance. Right and left do have major substantive disagreements about social issues, as well as the appropriate role of government in our lives, that can't be papered over by wishful thinking.

But by making peer-to-peer connections that obviate the need for intercession of an elite media who intuitively serve the interests of the Masters of the Universe, the structure of the internet could potentially facilitate the trans-partisan alliance of outsiders capable of taking on insiders on discrete issues.

When corporate money is limited in its ability to influence political outcomes on one side, it simply achieves its objectives by flowing to the other side. And as long as the online world reinforces the tribalism that perpetuates the problems of partisan politics, the results will be the same.

I do have hope. But in order to have any real, lasting impact, online activists are going to have to change both the language and the terms of the debates. None of us can win the battle against a heavily armed corporate world by ourselves. We're going to have to extricate ourselves, and our political dialogue, from the tribalism and demagoguery that facilitates corporate hegemony.

Because until we do, we are simply putting new tools in the service of the old order. And we will continue to lose.

Wikileaks Increases Transparency and Accountability in Democracies

William Quigley

William Quigley is the legal director for the Center for Constitutional Rights, a national legal and educational organization dedicated to advancing and defending the rights guaranteed by the United States Constitution and the Universal Declaration of Human Rights.

Since 9-11, the US government, through Presidents [George W.] Bush and [Barack] Obama, has increasingly told the US public that "state secrets" will not be shared with citizens. Candidate Obama pledged to reduce the use of state secrets, but President Obama continued the Bush tradition. The Courts and Congress and international allies have gone meekly along with the escalating secrecy demands of the US Executive.

By labeling tens of millions of documents secret, the US government has created a huge vacuum of information.

But information is the lifeblood of democracy. Information about government contributes to a healthy democracy. Transparency and accountability are essential elements of good government. Likewise, "a lack of government transparency and accountability undermines democracy and gives rise to cynicism and mistrust," according to a 2008 Harris survey commissioned by the Association of Government Accountants.

The Wikileaks Matter

Into the secrecy vacuum stepped Private Bradley Manning, who, according to the *Associated Press*, was able to defeat

"Pentagon security systems using little more than a Lady Gaga CD and a portable computer memory stick."

Manning apparently sent the information to Wikileaks—a non profit media organization, which specializes in publishing leaked information. Wikileaks in turn shared the documents to other media around the world including the *New York Times* and published much of it on its website.

Despite criminal investigations by the US and other governments, it is not clear that media organizations like Wikileaks can be prosecuted in the US in light of First Amendment Recall that the First Amendment says: "Congress shall make no law respecting an establishment of religion, or prohibiting the free exercise thereof; or abridging the freedom of speech, or of the press; or of the right of the people peaceably to assemble, and to petition the government for a redress of grievances."

Information is the lifeblood of democracy. Information about government contributes to a healthy democracy.

Outraged politicians are claiming that the release of government information is the criminal equivalent of terrorism and puts innocent people's lives at risk. Many of those same politicians authorized the modern equivalent of carpet bombing of Baghdad and other Iraqi cities, the sacrifice of thousands of lives of soldiers and civilians, and drone assaults on civilian areas in Afghanistan, Pakistan and Yemen. Their anger at a document dump, no matter how extensive, is more than a little suspect.

Good for Democracy

Everyone, including Wikileaks and the other media reporting the documents, hopes that no lives will be lost because of this. So far, that appears to be the case as *McClatchey Newspapers* reported November 28, 2010, that "US officials conceded that they have no evidence to date that the [prior] release of documents led to anyone's death."

Wikileaks has the potential to make transparency and accountability more robust in the US. That is good for democracy.

The US has been going in the wrong direction for years by classifying millions of documents as secrets. Wikileaks and other media which report these so called secrets will embarrass people yes. Wikileaks and other media will make leaders uncomfortable yes. But embarrassment and discomfort are small prices to pay for a healthier democracy.

Wikileaks has the potential to make transparency and accountability more robust in the US. That is good for democracy.

Political Campaigns Can Manipulate Social Media

Jared Keller

Jared Keller is an associate editor for The Atlantic, *a magazine that covers news and analysis on politics, business, culture, technology, and life. He has also written for* Lapham's Quarterly's *Deja Vu blog,* National Journal's *The Hotline,* Boston's *Weekly Dig, and* Preservation *magazine.*

Since young voters discovered they could friend Barack Obama on Facebook during the 2008 election, social media has become ingrained in the way we think about political discourse. Politicians and tech evangelists alike see it as the key to a new type of politics: Campaigns and candidates can better engage citizens, facilitate grassroots organization, and craft legislation with the direct input of a Tweeting electorate. The inevitable results, optimists argue, will be a sort of "digital democracy," defined by a closer, more coherent relationship between the elected officials and their constituents.

But social media, like any tool, can be used to erode democratic practices as well.

A few days before the special election in Massachusetts to fill Senate seat formerly held by the late Edward Kennedy, the conservative American Future Fund (AFF) conducted a "Twitter-bomb" campaign against Attorney General Martha Coakley, the Democratic candidate. The AFF set up nine anonymous Twitter accounts in early morning hours prior to the election that sent hundred of tweets accusing Martha Coakley of taking money from health insurance lobbyists to other influential Twitter accounts around the state, linking back to anonymous websites containing further details. Twitter realized the messages were spam and shut down the accounts two hours later, but by that point the messages had reached nearly 60,000 people. The sudden spike caused the attacks on Coakley to turn up in Google searches for her name, effectively gaming Google's real-time search functions. Scott Brown won the election due to a variety of factors, but Eni Mustafaraj and Panagiotis Metaxes of Wellseley College, who documented the incident, concluded that the promulgation of anti-Coakley messages through social networks highlighted future opportunities for "a small fraction of the population to hijack the trustworthiness of a search engine and propagate their messages to a huge audience for free, with little effort, and without trace." While the attacks on Coakley were based on a fundraiser she did indeed hold in Washington, hosted by lobbyists with health care clients, it's plausible the same methods could be used to spread blatant misinformation about a candidate.

More recently, a group of right-leaning users on the popular social news network Digg were accused of censoring from the site stories with a perceived liberal bias and promoting stories with a conservative slant through collective action. While the online identities of many of the so-called "Digg Patriots" were revealed, their motivations and affiliations with existing political organizations remain subject to speculation. "In a time when mainstream news organizations have already ceded a substantial chunk of their opinion-shaping influence to Web-based partisans on the left and right, does each side now feel entitled to its own facts as well?" asked Michael Hirschorn with regard to the Digg Patriots. "And thanks to the emergence of social media as the increasingly dominant mode of information dissemination, are we nearing a time when truth itself will become just another commodity to be bought and sold on the social-media markets?"

More troubling is the possibility that the story of the American Future Fund could become a common anecdote during election years. While electoral watchdogs focused on the flow of corporate resources into campaigns around the country during this past cycle, social media may prove the next hot topic in years to come. If the infiltration and manipulation of influential search engines and social networks is so simple, could social media eventually pose enough of a problem that we need laws and regulations to govern its use in campaigns?

Filippo Menczer, Associate Professor of Informatics and Computer Science at the Indiana University, Bloomington, serves as the principal investigator for Truthy, a research project devoted to tracking the spread of memes online. Named after Stephen Colbert's from-the-gut "truthiness," the Truthy team uses an algorithm based on election-specific keywords and mood indicators—a type of sentiment analysis very similar to the one used at the University of Indiana to predict changes in the stock market—to follow political misinformation campaigns on Twitter. The Truthy team, inspired by the Massachusetts election, decided to track digital astroturf campaigns during election years.

"We have a 90 percent success rate at tracking this sort of abnormal behavior on social networks, and it happens frequently" says Menczer. "People are being manipulated without realizing it because a meme can be given instant global popularity by a high search engine ranking, in turn perpetuating a falsehood."

"If you think about how much putting an ad on TV costs, you could pay an army of people to post fake information and promote it through social networks," says Menczer, who, based on his research, anticipates future manipulation of the Twittersphere for political gains. "It's a form of information pollution. Spamming on social networks has very low cost and has the potential to influence a large amount of people. From the point of view of someone running for office, it would be crazy NOT to use this system."

Accountability is a huge problem in the social media sphere, where anonymity is still easy to maintain. "If anything, this is in violation of Twitter terms of service . . . but so what? You can just make another account. There's no accountability," says Menczer. "I think it's scary. It's extremely easy to fabricate news [and] use these methods to manipulate the Web because people want to believe what they want to believe."

Much of social media remains untouched by campaign finance and transparency laws, and the Federal Election Commission (FEC), which is seen by campaign legal experts as reluctant to regulate, does not seem eager to make new rules for the Web. Currently, social media is regarded as another subset of Internet communications; in 2006, the Federal Elections Commission concluded that finance laws apply to web advertisements and messages that appear on the sites of political organizations, but beyond those two categories, other types of Web-based activities go ungoverned by and large by federal law.

Accountability is a huge problem in the social media sphere, where anonymity is still easy to maintain.

But campaign finance law in general regulates spending money in an effort to influence elections, and a coordinated effort to employ social media strategists would potentially come under federal purview, requiring that campaigns disclose who they're paying and what they're paying for, which could expose the inner workings of a surreptitious social media operations and provide more accountability for voters trying to navigate a sea of information pollution.

"The operative terms here are 'hiring' or 'paying' influencers in the social space," says Paul Ryan, associate legal counsel and FEC program director at the Campaign Legal Center in Washington, DC. "When big money changes hands, there's reason to regulate that activity, whatever it may be; the fact that it happens on the Internet doesn't really distinguish it from anything else. The way campaign finance law deals with Facebook is that I'm free to say whatever I want. I have a couple of hundreds of friends and while I may have a capacity to influence my friends' decisions in elections, I don't spend money and I don't sponsor status updates. But if I buy advertising from Facebook, federal laws do encompass that activity and justifiably so."

But in terms of the necessary conditions for disclosure, social media still exists in something of a gray area. "There is no requirement that a blogger who is also on a campaign payroll as a consultant disclose anything on a personal blog," Ryan tells me. "They would have to disclose with a 'paid for' if they are paid specifically to disseminate a particular message. But with things like blogs and social media, readers may not get a clear indication as to exactly whether a message is coming from a person as a personal blogger or as a paid consultant."

With the potential power and legal ambiguity surrounding social media in the election cycle, many anticipate a rise in future usage.

Ryan provides the example of White House Counsel Bob Bauer, who, prior to serving as the general counsel for Obama For America in 2008, wrote a blog about campaign finance law as an attorney. "There are a lot of other lawyers who blog about lawyers who work on money and politics issues and election law, and we have to ask: Are they doing so wearing their hat as working for a client or not?" says Ryan. "It's easier to track with lawyers who bill their hours. There are political consultants who wear a lot of different hats." In short, a staffer could plausibly run a coordinated spamming attack like that used in the Massachusetts election while claiming that it's something done while wearing the hat of a private citizen, rather than that of a paid staffer.

With the potential power and legal ambiguity surrounding social media in the election cycle, many anticipate a rise in future usage. "We expect that, unless addressed by the search engines, this practice will intensify during the next congressional elections in 2010," wrote Mustafarj and Metaxes in their report following Scott Brown's victory in Massachusetts. Filippo Menczer sees more coherent foundations for digital electioneering in place. "Sites like [the Heritage Foundation's] http:// noenergytax.com/ are making astroturf into a 'fun' game where you compete for how much volume you generate in promoting a certain view (in this particular case it is opposition to cap & trade legislation, but it could be any policy issue)," Menczer wrote in an e-mail. "Social media consultants like DAG make the process easy and semi-automated. We're seeing instances of using crowd-sourcing to mass-create Twitter accounts; while this may or may not have been done by political activists, the door is open."

Many Web Users Say the Internet Increases the Influence of Extremists

Katie Kindelan

Katie Kindelan is a writer who writes frequently for Social Times, *an online magazine, and who resides in the Washington, DC area.*

A new study has found that one in five adults who use the Internet turned to social networks to get or share information about the 2010 midterm elections. So when a voter turns to Facebook instead of a candidate's website for information, is that a win or a loss for democracy?

Going Online for Political Information

In the study, released this week by the Pew Research Center, researchers confirmed what politicians, and campaign consultants, have long known: given the opportunity to interact with people rather than institutions, people look to connect to those they trust, i.e. friends, family and colleagues.

But now in the age of social media and the Internet, like never before, they have an outlet, and a means, to collect the information they want, when they want it.

"The take-away from this political election is that these online spaces—whether they are social-media tools, online news sources or blogs— . . . are now part of the standard tool kit for people engaged with politics," said Aaron Smith, the report's author and a senior research specialist at Pew Internet.

Nearly three-quarters (73 percent) of American Internet users, or 54 percent of all voters, went online in 2010 for news or information about the midterm elections or to communicate with others about the campaigns, according to the report.

That makes the 2010 races the second consecutive election, and first ever mid-term race, in which the Pew Research Center's Internet & American Life Project found more than half of all adults using the Internet for political activism and to gather information, from watching a political video to fact-checking and sharing and discussing information.

And the information voters are getting online, appears to have sway.

Just over one-third of respondents said the information they saw online made them decide to vote for or against a particular candidate.

Those results underscore the important role that technology, but, more specifically, social networks like Twitter and Facebook, will play in the 2012 presidential campaign, the report concluded.

"As more people live more of their lives in the social web, it becomes an important space for them to share their views and interpret what is going on in the world around them."

Nearly three-quarters (73 percent) of American Internet users, or 54 percent of all voters, went online in 2010 for news or information about the midterm elections.

The Downside

Yet, while 61 percent of adults surveyed said the Internet exposed people to a wider range of political views than they might get from traditional news media sources, they also remained skeptical about the quality and value of the information they were finding.

The report found that 56 percent of Internet users believe it is usually difficult to differentiate information they find on the Internet that is true from information that is not true.

And, at the same time, 55 percent of all Web users feel that the Internet increases the influence of those with extreme political views, compared with 30 percent who say that the Internet reduces the influence of those with extreme views because it gives people a chance to be heard.

Fifty-five percent of all Web users feel that the Internet increases the influence of those with extreme political views.

"People recognize that there's a downside," said Smith. "They sort of see it on a broader level, where they have concerns that the Internet promotes extremism . . . but they think it has value for them personally, and they are not falling into those kinds of things."

Wikileaks Uses the Internet to Illegally Inflict Harm

Philip J. Crowley

Philip J. Crowley is an assistant secretary of state at the Bureau of Public Affairs, part of the US State Department.

What I do every day is to enunciate the United States Government view on world affairs. As events permit, I look to see if we can find some humor in a situation. When President [Barack] Obama was selected to receive the Nobel Prize, I said it was better to have these kinds of accolades thrown our way than shoes. When President Hugo Chavez suggested Venezuela would pursue a space program, I suggested he stick with terrestrial rather than extraterrestrial pursuits. President Chavez called me ridiculous—by name—high praise indeed. The other day, Iran invited diplomats from a handful of countries, but not the United States, to visit some nuclear facilities as an alternative to full cooperation with the International Atomic Energy Agency. I termed it the Magical Mystery Tour.

Today we use a variety of media to communicate to governments and people around the world—formal briefings that are covered by traditional media, as well as social media to bypass governments and communicate directly with people. And [MSNBC reporters] Chuck Todd and Savannah Guthrie late last year recognized me for the Tweet of the Year, in part because they couldn't believe the State Department Spokesman actually had a sense of humor.

After President [Jimmy] Carter traveled to Pyongyang to rescue an American citizen jailed there, following President Clinton who brought home two journalists the year before, I tweeted that the American people should heed our travel warnings. After all, we only have so many former Presidents. In a shameless attempt at self-promotion—I am currently hundreds of followers behind our UN ambassador and my friend, Susan Rice—feel free to follow me @pjcrowley.

Importance of a Free and Vibrant Press

In my view, success in the 21st Century depends on effective governance. A free and vibrant press plays an important role around the world in the development of civil society and accountable governments. As a general rule, the freer the press, the more transparent and more democratic the government is likely to be. In the context of this seminar, Media and Politics, think of the places around the world recently where existing governments are clearly guilty of substantial election fraud, fraud that either skewed the results to a significant degree, or stole elections outright. This involves the election in Iran in June 2009, where the government harassed the traditional media as they covered the election and the fraud that was evident, as well as the opposition that very effectively used social media during the campaign, and has refused to be silenced to the present day.

Dictatorships understand the power of the media, where in Burma, the ruling junta held an election in November [2010] for which it refused to allow Aung San Suu Kyi to participate, nor allowed outside media to cover. The result was a kind of election laundering, where the existing military government attempted to use the election to transform itself into a civilian government. But it lacks the legitimacy that only civil society, backed by a vibrant press, can bestow. Unfortunately there is no shortage of present-day examples, from Cote d'Ivoire to Belarus, where the media continues to document the actions of repressive governments that in one case refuses to accept the results of an election that it did not expect to lose, and in the other has literally jailed every opposition figure that dared run against Europe's last dictator.

The former Yugoslavia is my best example of a case where the investment in independent media helped to transform a country and we hope over time a region, contributing to the dynamic that led to the end of the rule of Slobodan Milosevic, and his transfer to The Hague where he died in prison while facing charges for crimes against humanity. We also know that the media can be used to incite ethnic violence, as we saw tragically in the 1990s in Rwanda. We continue to have concerns regarding state-controlled, particularly in the Middle East, that continue to foment religious tension across the region.

No one is a greater advocate for a vibrant independent and responsible press, committed to the promotion of freedom of expression and development of a true global civil society, than the United States. Every day, we express concern about the plight of journalists (or bloggers) around the world who are intimidated, jailed or even killed by governments that are afraid of their people, and afraid of the empowerment that comes with the free flow of information within a civil society.

Most recently, we did so in the context of Tunisia, which has hacked social media accounts while claiming to protect their citizens from the incitement of violence. But in doing so, we feel the government is unduly restricting the ability of its people to peacefully assemble and express their views in order to influence government policies. These are universal principles that we continue to support. And we practice what we preach. Just look at our own country and cable television. We don't silence dissidents. We make them television news analysts.

The Wikileaks Matter

Some in the human rights community in this country, and around the world, are questioning our commitment to freedom of expression, freedom of the press and Internet freedom in the aftermath of WikiLeaks. I am constrained in what I can say, both because individual cables remain classified, and the leak is under investigation by the Department of Justice. But let me briefly put this in context and then I will open things up for questions. WikiLeaks is about the unauthorized disclosure of classified information. It is not an exercise in Internet freedom. It is about the legitimate investigation of a crime. It is about the need to continue to protect sensitive information while enabling the free flow of public information.

WikiLeaks is about the unauthorized disclosure of classified information. It is not an exercise in Internet freedom.

We remain arguably the most transparent society in the world. The American people, through innovations including C-SPAN, are a well-informed citizenry, which is crucial to a functioning democracy. We can have a discussion about how well our democracy is functioning, and whether political figures are spending more time pandering or posturing on television than actually governing. . . .

This transparency relies upon a vibrant independent fourth estate that serves as a vital check and balance in our democracy. The First Amendment created deliberate tension in the relationship between the media and government. This tension helps to sustain effective oversight of government. When I stand up each day and answer questions about U.S. policy and actions, in a small way, I am part of this process where government is accountable to its people. And, trust me, the system works. I have the fan mail to prove it, particularly when I appear on FOX. Some FOX viewers now have me on speed dial.

Transparency does not mean there are no secrets. Whether you are a government or a business, there is proprietary information that is vital to your day-to-day function. Coca-Cola has its secret formula. Google has its search algorithm. Their success is based on these secrets. As a government, we are no different. In the conduct of our diplomacy, we have confidential interactions around the world every day. These conversations, with government officials, civil society activists, business people and journalists, help us make sense of the world and inform our policy-making. These confidential exchanges are rooted in our values and serve our national interest. They are based on mutual trust, trust that the confidence will not be betrayed.

Someone inside our government violated their sworn oath to protect the national interest and protect classified and sensitive information that is an inherent part of the conduct of our national security policy. We can debate whether there are too many secrets, but no one should doubt that there has been substantial damage in the unauthorized release of a database containing, among other things, 251,000 State Department cables, many of them classified.

Transparency does not mean there are no secrets. Whether you are a government or a business, there is proprietary information that is vital to your day-to-day function.

Real Lives and Interests Compromised

We have encountered leaks before, and worked through them. We will do so in this case as well. But this case is different, in its volume and scope. Unlike the past, where someone might have smuggled out a document or file about one subject and given it to one reporter, in this case, the database contained documents that touched every part of the world, every relationship we have around the world and almost national interest. The reaction has varied country by country, but human nature being what it is, there will be impact for at least a time. Governments will be more cautious in sharing sensitive information. Why is this important? It was the sharing of information last year that enabled the United States, working with other governments, to intercept a plot to blow up cargo aircraft over Chicago. If less information is shared in the future, our policies and our actions could be less effective.

The release of this information has placed hundreds of people at risk, in many cases the very civil society activists that WikiLeaks has suggested it wants to empower around the world. We interact regularly with people in all walks of life who are trying to reform repressive societies, both inside and outside government. In some cases, their names have been withheld, but many have been exposed and are now at risk. The mere fact that classified documents now reside in unclassified and less secure databases means that this information can be intercepted by a foreign security service. So the fact that only 2,700 documents have been publicly released is small comfort to the people who have been needlessly exposed.

We are tracking hundreds of people around the world who we believe, in one way or another, are now in danger—reaching out to as many as we prudently can and helping ensure to the extent we can that they remain safe. The founder of WikiLeaks has claimed that no one has lost his or her life due to these releases. That is true as far as we know, but that is not the only measure of the impact.

Real lives and real interests have been compromised by what has been done here. We are doing everything we can to mitigate that impact, but as the Secretary of State said this week, it will take years to move beyond it.

Responsible Internet Freedom

We are a nation of laws, and the laws of our country have been violated. Since we function under the rule of law, it is appropriate and necessary that we investigate and prosecute those who have violated US law. Some have suggested that the ongoing investigation marks a retreat from our commitment to freedom of expression, freedom of the press and Internet freedom. Nonsense.

These are universal principles and our commitment is unwavering. These freedoms have always coexisted with the rule of law and the application of laws is in no way intended to deny access to readily available information or silence legitimate and necessary political discourse. But our belief in Internet freedom does not include the right to use the Internet to illegally inflict harm. We must exercise these rights responsibly.

WikiLeaks reminds us of the on-going challenge of how to protect vital information, whether personal or classified information, while also promoting the free flow of information that can empower people to form global communities and change the world for the better. We believe it is possible and necessary to do both.

CHAPTER 3

Have Social Media Been Instrumental in Promoting Recent Revolutions?

Chapter Overview

Sean Aday, Henry Farrell, Marc Lynch, John Sides, John Kelly, and Ethan Zuckerman

Sean Aday is an associate professor of media and public affairs and international affairs at George Washington University, as well as director of the Institute for Public Diplomacy and Global Communication. Henry Farrell is an associate professor of political science at George Washington University. Marc Lynch is an associate professor of political science and international affairs at George Washington University and director of the Institute for Middle East Studies. John Sides is an assistant professor of political science at George Washington University. John Kelly is the founder and lead scientist at Morningside Analytics and an affiliate of the Berkman Center for Internet and Society at Harvard University. Ethan Zuckerman is senior researcher at the Berkman Center for Internet and Society at Harvard University and also part of Global Voices, a group of international bloggers bridging cultural and linguistic differences through weblogs.

In January 2010, U.S. Secretary of State Hillary Clinton articulated a powerful vision of the Internet as promoting freedom and global political transformation and rewriting the rules of political engagement and action. Her vision resembles that of others who argue that new media technologies facilitate participatory politics and mass mobilization, help promote democracy and free markets, and create new kinds of global citizens. Some observers have even suggested that Twitter's creators should receive the Nobel Peace Prize for their role in the 2009 Iranian protests. But not everyone has such sanguine views. Clinton herself was careful to note when sharing her vision that new media were not an "unmitigated blessing." Pessimists argue that these technologies may actually exacerbate conflict, as exemplified in Kenya, the Czech Republic, and Uganda, and help authoritarian regimes monitor and police their citizens. They argue that new media encourage self-segregation and polarization as people seek out only information that reinforces their prior beliefs, offering ever more opportunities for the spread of hate, misinformation, and prejudice. Some skeptics question whether new media have significant effects at all. Perhaps they are simply a tool used by those who would protest in any event or a trendy "hook" for those seeking to tell political stories. Do new media have real consequences for contentious politics—and in which direction?

Anecdotes and Intuition

The sobering answer is that, fundamentally, no one knows. To this point, little research has sought to estimate the causal effects of new media in a methodologically rigorous fashion, or to gather the rich data needed to establish causal influence. Without rigorous research designs or rich data, partisans of all viewpoints turn to anecdotal evidence and intuition. It seems improbable that such a massive change in political communication would not matter, even if the data to demonstrate the effects are lacking and older forms of political communication and mass media continue to shape political outcomes. Former British prime minister Gordon Brown has suggested that new media can actually prevent genocide: "You cannot have Rwanda again because information would come out far more quickly about what is actually going on and the public opinion would grow to the point where action would need to be taken." Perhaps, but Michael Jackson's death drove discussion of Uighur protests against the Chinese government off Twitter, and new media have paid little attention to ongoing strife in the Congo. Even coverage of the devastating 2010 earthquake in Haiti had real problems. The earthquake was a top-trending topic on Twitter, which allowed millions to get information, and even to put pressure on the U.S. Air Force to allow relief flights into the Port-au-Prince airport. However, mainstream media outlets may have benefited more from Twitter than ordinary citizens.

The answers to these questions have important consequences for politics and policy. The Internet could be a powerful force for political freedom. To harness its power, Secretary Clinton has argued, the United States must "put these tools in the hands of people around the world who will use them to advance democracy and human rights, fight climate change and epidemics, build global support for President Obama's goal of a world without nuclear weapons, and encourage sustainable economic development." Similarly, a growing number of analysts argue that supporting Internet freedom is crucial to bringing about regime change in Iran, as access to information and the freedom to connect will empower the Green Movement against the current regime.

Former British prime minister Gordon Brown has suggested that new media can actually prevent genocide....

But these assumptions, however plausible, remain largely untested. Will a freer Internet empower the Green Movement in Iran or will it simply allow the incumbent regime to dominate a new terrain? To make good policy, policymakers and advocates need to understand not only who is winning and who is losing, but *why* one side is winning or losing. This requires much more systematic thinking about the relationship between new media and politics. If new media change the politics of unrest, revolution, violence, and civil war, then governments and civil society need to understand how, so as to better respond to events as they are happening. If certain patterns of communication are associated with a greater likelihood of violence, then these patterns must be identified as far in advance as possible. If greater access to information technology makes violence less likely, then technology policy must be integrated into the standard toolkits for conflict prevention and democracy promotion. . . .

Social Media Gave Iranian Protestors a Voice

Mark Pfeifle

Mark Pfeifle was deputy national security adviser for strategic communications and global outreach at the National Security Council from 2007 to 2009.

The video gave substance to what seemed so far away. We saw the look in her eyes as they went lifeless. We heard the sounds of her friends and family as they begged her to hold on. And she became the personification of the struggle for democracy in a country where voices for freedom are quelled.

Her name was Neda Agha-Soltan, and without Twitter we might never have known that she lived in Iran, that she dreamed of a free Iran, and that she died in a divided Iran for her dreams.

Neda became the voice of a movement; Twitter became the megaphone. Twitter is a free social-messaging utility. It drove people around the world to pictures, videos, sound bites, and blogs in a true reality show of life, dreams, and death. Last month's marches [June 2009] for freedom and the violent crackdowns were not only documented but personalized into a story of mythic tragedy.

When traditional journalists were forced to leave the country. Twitter became a window for the world to view hope, heroism, and horror. It became the assignment desk, the reporter, and the producer. And, because of this, Twitter and its creators are worthy of being considered for the Nobel Peace Prize.

Twitter's Role in the Iranian Protests

I first mentioned this idea while being interviewed on a cable news program. Many scoffed. That's understandable. But think about what Twitter has accomplished: It has empowered people to attempt to resolve a domestic showdown with international implications—and has enabled the world to stand with them. It laid the foundation to pressure the world to denounce oppression in Iran.

Twitter has been criticized as a time-waster—a way for people to inform their friends about the minutiae of their lives, 140 characters at a time. But in the past month, 140 characters were enough to shine a light on Iranian oppression and elevate Twitter to the level of change agent. Even the government of Iran has been forced to utilize the very tool they attempted to squelch to try to hold on to power.

Without Twitter, the world might have known little more than a losing candidate accusing the powers that be of alleged fraud. Without Twitter, the people of Iran would not have felt empowered and confident to stand up for freedom and democracy. They did so because they knew the world was watching. With Twitter, they now shout hope with a passion and dedication that resonates not just with those on their street, but with millions across the globe.

Twitter . . . laid the foundation to pressure the world to denounce oppression in Iran.

Other social media have certainly played an important part in giving freedom a voice. Iranian presidential candidate Mir Hossein Mousavi has amassed more than 100,000 supporters on Facebook. At the height of the protest activities, according to Mashable.com's Ben Parr, more than 221,000 Iran tweets were sent in one hour. In one day, 3,000 Iranian videos were uploaded on YouTube, and 2.2 million blog entries were posted.

But Twitter's role has been unique. More so than other networks, it offers many more users the opportunity to communicate ideas, text, and media. On most other sites, only people who have accepted one another as "friends" are able to read updates. Via "hashtags" (for example, #iranelection), Twitter overcomes this barrier, allowing people interested in a particular subject to tweet and retweet messages. Additionally, through cellphone applications and SMS, Twitter proves easier to update—and harder for an oppressive regime to block— than other types of social media.

Although we don't know how the uprising in Iran will end, or where the symbols of freedom and liberty will again be given power by people who require an unfettered means of communicating with the rest of us, Twitter and other social media outlets have become the soft weapons of democracy. Twitter told us the story of Neda's supreme sacrifice. It is telling the story of the Iranian people yearning to breathe free. For those reasons, Twitter deserves consideration for the Nobel Peace Prize.

Social Media Have Been Powerful Tools in Organizing Egypt's Revolution

S. Craig Watkins

S. Craig Watkins, an associate professor at the University of Texas at Austin, studies and writes about young people's social and digital media behaviors. He is the author of the 2009 book, The Young and the Digital: What the Migration to Social Network Sites, Games, and Anytime, Anywhere Media Means for Our Future.

In the wake of the uprising that shook up Egypt and ended the thirty year regime of Hosni Mubarak a growing debate around the role of social media has ensued. The press, looking for catchy headlines characterized the uprising as "the first Twitter revolution," or "Facebook revolution." Conversely, a number of critics and academics cry foul proclaiming that people, not technology, conducted the revolution.

Anyone who has even a pedestrian understanding of social movements knows that they are often caused by the convergence of social, economic, cultural, and political factors. And this is certainly true in the Arab world. Decades of government corruption, elite economic self-interest, the arrogance of power, and historic economic inequalities were the primary catalyst for what *Newsweek* magazine called, "a youthquake that is rocking the Arab world."

A recent tweet by former U.S. Secretary of Labor Robert Reich is subtle but profound: "We cannot in good conscience continue to reward the rich, penalize the poor, and ignore the middle. There will be a day of reckoning." While Reich was referring to the current political and economic climate in the U.S. the tweet speaks to the wider global condition. While social media was not the catalyst of the Egyptian protest it was certainly a tool for mobilizing protest.

The five million Facebook accounts in Egypt make it the second most popular site in the country. YouTube is the third most visited site. Whereas protestors used Facebook to organize, set dates, and "peercast," that is, share mobile pictures and video with peers, Twitter became the social media backbone of the movement's day-to-day machinations.

While social media was not the catalyst of the Egyptian protest it was certainly a tool for mobilizing protest.

A First Hand View of the Protests

I recently had a chance to speak with a young man who made Tahrir Square his home during parts of the uprising.

Karim (this is a pseudonym) studies social media and told me that he felt like he was participating in history. On February 5 [2011] he sent me a number of pictures from his Facebook album that captured various aspects of the massive demonstrations in Egypt. The pictures, of course, had an ethnographic aesthetic about them and offer a much more intimate perspective of the movement than did the highly selected images most people viewed on television. The Facebook album included pictures of people protesting, confronting the police, nurturing the wounded, laughing, celebrating, and, most important, bonding together in a common cause to transform their country. In many of the pictures I also noticed people capturing the protest with their mobile devices.

In literally thousands of instances they streamed pictures, videos, tweets, and Facebook updates for their comrades around Egypt and the world. This kind of media production is a hallmark feature of the digital media age. Egyptian protestors were not only consuming images of their efforts, they were also producing and sharing those images with the world and giving new meaning to the notion of participatory politics.

Karim explained the popularity of photos this way. "As you might know, sometimes these demonstrations are not safe; so, as soon as we reach Tahrir Square, we take photos of the demonstration and upload them to our Facebook profiles to tell our friends that we are participating and encourage them to come over."

Curious about the adoption of technology in the uprisings, I asked Karim how did social media influence the events in Egypt. Karim replied that, "the demonstration started on January 25 and the call for it was done mainly through Facebook." Facebook emerged, in part, as an efficient way to coordinate and organize protestors. The first Facebook post related directly to the events in February was made on January 14 at 11:18 pm, eleven days before the first massive protests in Tahrir Square. The main tag simply read: . . . (Rough) Translation: "Message to the people of Egypt: Let the January 25 is the torch of change in Egypt."

According to Karim, social media was crucial from the outset of the movement because it gave people on the ground an information technology that they could control. "Because of the government's heavy control over all the traditional media," he explained, "the Internet is the only available option for all opposition parties and movements." That is also why after two days of protest the government shut down the internet and mobile phone service. Determined to keep the momentum people used everything from dial-up modems to proxy-servers.

The Role of Twitter

The first and what will likely go down in history as one of the most famous Twitter hashtag's in the Egyptian revolution was

"#jan25," created by a twenty-one year-old woman who goes by the Twitter name, @alya1989262. Follow the "#jan25" feed (created January 15, one day after the above Facebook announcement) and one of the most striking features is the range and complexity of communication that took place via Twitter. In many ways, Twitter became the mediated eyes, ears, and voice of the day-to-day life of the protest.

#jan25 is, in essence, a transcript of history, a log not merely of what people were tweeting, but what they were thinking and, most important, doing. Twitter was used in a variety of ways during the protest. At times it was used as a tool for real time communication between protesters, informing each other about the location of police, where protestors should go, and what media around the world were saying about the events on the ground. According to @alya1989262, Twitter, "most importantly, allow[ed] us to share on the ground info like police brutality, things to watch out for, activists getting arrested, etc."

> *Twitter and Facebook did not start the revolution but they did help generations of Egyptians realize a world that not that long ago would have been impossible to imagine.*

Twitter was also used to rally, recruit, and encourage people to come out and show their solidarity with the protestors. In other instances it was used as a broadcast medium, a technology that allowed the protesters to tell their side of the story, their side of history. In societies where freedom of the press is severely constrained and the press is often the mouthpiece of the government, social media emerges as an alternative broadcasting platform, a way to communicate and connect with the world. There is historical precedence for this.

In the 1960s leaders of the U.S. civil rights movement came to understand the power of television and how the images of police brutality turned the tide against the state sanctioned southern hostility toward freedom fighters and their demands for political equality. In the student led movement against the Vietnam War chants like "the whole world is watching" revealed an effort to leverage the power of television to mobilize widespread support for their social movement. By staying connected to Twitter the protestors in Egypt were also able to track how well their efforts were trending beyond home. What did they see? The whole world really was watching them but this time on YouTube, Facebook, Twitter, and other social media platforms in addition to television, @alya1989262 acknowledged this, "Twitter trends also help us gauge how visible we are to the international community." What makes social movements in the age of social media so distinct is the real time nature of communication in the execution of protest as well as the ability to share perspectives, narratives, and experiences that establish an ambient connection to the outside world.

As we gain a better understanding of what happened in Egypt and other parts of the Arab world we will also learn more about who used mobile devices and social media to energize their efforts to create democratic freedoms. Karim contends that, "the youth who called for the first demonstration on January 25 belong to upper middle class in Egypt and most of them, if not all, have Internet access." @alya1989262's account is similar. "A certain class of activists are armed with smartphones, which allow them to live-tweet the protests." Does this suggest that the movement was ignited by a generation of tech savvy and college educated citizens? Not necessarily. But the idea of this segment rising up to confront power is not all that surprising when you consider their condition. Roughly a third of the population in the middle east is under thirty and a noteworthy percentage of them have college degrees. The young and the digital in the middle east are connected to the world in a way that previous generations could not even have imagined. And yet, the unemployment rate of young college educated persons in the middle east is staggeringly high. A recent report from NPR [National Public Radio] notes that 40% of young persons with college degrees in Saudia Arabia, for example, are unemployed. Faced with the prospects of a life with few if any meaningful opportunities to utilize their cultural capital—education—many young people realized that they had nothing to lose by confronting the [Egyptian President Hosni] Mubarak regime.

What happened in Egypt is yet another confirmation of what our research has consistently demonstrated regarding young people's engagement with social media: young people use social media not as a substitute for face-to-face interactions with their peers and the world but rather as a complement. Young people in Egypt did not use social media to avoid gathering with each other or to passively participate in their country's revolution. They used it to encourage gathering with each other for the expressed purpose of actively participating in the revolution. Twitter and Facebook did not start the revolution but they did help generations of Egyptians realize a world that not that long ago would have been impossible to imagine.

Social Media Have Played a Significant Role in Various Middle East Protests

Erik Sass

Erik Sass is a journalist from Los Angeles who writes about the media industry.

The argument over the role of social media in the revolutions which shook the Middle East over the last two months [January and February 2011] has meandered along in that particularly unsatisfying way that public debates tend to nowadays, with pundits lobbing generalities in online echo chambers unlikely to produce any decisive conclusion, with scant evidence that anyone is even listening to the other "side." Indeed, I would be hard pressed to identify the central issue or issues of this disjointed non-dialogue at this point, after all the straw men have been duly demolished: does anyone seriously believe that social media made the revolutions all by itself, no humans required? And at the same time, is anyone seriously arguing social media didn't play a significant role?

Gladwell's Unfounded Arguments

Well, yes: Malcolm Gladwell appears to be arguing just that, with oblivious confidence and despite mounting evidence to the contrary, apparently out of perverse intellectual pride. You see, Gladwell painted himself into a rhetorical corner with a mildly infamous essay in *The New Yorker*, asserting that social media has not, will not, and cannot change the face of true social activism—meaning the kind of confrontations with unjust authority which may lead to violence and personal injury.

After the upheavals in Tunisia, Egypt, and Libya, many observers (including myself) seized on the role of social media to refute Gladwell's sweeping dismissal of its revolutionary potential. Safe inside his fortress of paint, Gladwell has fired back on a couple occasions—but with arguments that are so unreflective, facile, and silly I almost have to wonder if he's putting us on.

[Malcolm Gladwell asserts] that social media has not, will not, and cannot change the face of true social activism.

The most recent riposte appears in the March–April issue of *Foreign Affairs*, where Gladwell contributed a short piece taking the "con" position on the issue of social media in revolution, versus Clay Shirky, who argued "pro." Once again, Gladwell tries to use historical analogies to make an embarrassingly simpleminded argument: basically, because revolutions happened in the past without social media, social media didn't play a role in the current Middle East revolutions.

No, really, that's what he's saying: "The lesson here is just because innovations in communications technology happen does not mean that they matter. . . . What evidence is there that social revolutions in the pre-Internet era suffered from a lack of cutting-edge communications and organizational tools?"

Lessons of History

Presuming Gladwell isn't joking, I would offer this response: no one ever said that social revolutions in the pre-Internet era suffered from such a lack. Indeed, that's kind of the whole point: every successful revolution has made use of the most advanced communications available at the time, which often (but not always) allowed rebels to outwit sclerotic governments which were behind the technological times.

During the American Revolution, patriots used secret printing presses hidden in basements; doesn't it seem significant that Benjamin Franklin, the father of Independence, was a printer by trade? During the French Revolution, the Directory organized the first draft in history with printed posters bearing the famous proclamation of a *levee en masse* on August 23, 1793. When communications advanced, revolutionaries were always among the earliest adopters: daily newspapers played a central role during the "liberal revolutions" of 1848— the British Library has a special collection devoted to them. During the Russian Revolution and ensuing civil war, control of telephones and telegraphs was crucial to the success of [Vladimir] Lenin's Bolsheviks, and a decade later Adolf Hitler pioneered the use of radio in politics (as these two examples illustrate, it's not always a good thing). Or how about Russian intellectual dissidents circulating photocopied samizdat texts in the Soviet Union in the 1960s and 1970s . . . or Ayatollah Khomeini's followers in Iran circulating audio tapes of his speeches against the Shah . . . and the list goes on—yes, right up to 2011, when an Egyptian man decides to name his newborn daughter "Facebook" in gratitude for the social network's role in the recent revolution.

Every successful revolution has made use of the most advanced communications available at the time.

The most embarrassing part of Gladwell's argument in *Foreign Affairs* is his attempt to use a more recent analogy which effectively refutes itself:

> I was reminded of a trip I took just over ten years ago, during the dot-com bubble. I went to the catalog clothier Lands' End in Wisconsin, determined to write about how the rise of the Internet and e-commerce was transforming retail. What I learned was that it was not.

Uh, really? Did I really just see Malcolm Gladwell, the Smarty-pants-in-chief, reach back a decade for a single anecdote proving that e-commerce hasn't "transformed" retail? Sorry, this is beyond embarrassing—it's just dumb. First of all, it may be worth noting that total e-commerce sales have climbed over 400% from $32.6 billion in 2001 to $165.4 billion in 2010, increasing from 1% to 5.5% of total retail sales. And oh yeah, as for Land's End, Information Week reports that "most of its revenue flows through its Web site today." So there's that.

I'm not just quibbling with Gladwell about one stupid anecdote: the fact is this mindset pervades his whole argument about social media. Shockingly, he seems to discount the idea of historical progression: it seems elementary that just because something didn't use to be important, doesn't mean it isn't important now, right? But that's exactly the argument he has made about social media, both in his *New Yorker* article and his subsequent defenses of it.

Social Media Promote Weak Ties, Not High-Risk Activism

Malcolm Gladwell

Malcolm Gladwell is an author and a writer for the New Yorker, *a weekly magazine of politics and culture.*

At four-thirty in the afternoon on Monday, February 1, 1960, four college students sat down at the lunch counter at the Woolworth's in downtown Greensboro, North Carolina. They were freshmen at North Carolina A. & T., a black college a mile or so away.

"I'd like a cup of coffee, please," one of the four, Ezell Blair, said to the waitress.

"We don't serve Negroes here," she replied.

The Woolworth's lunch counter was a long L-shaped bar that could seat sixty-six people, with a standup snack bar at one end. The seats were for whites. The snack bar was for blacks. Another employee, a black woman who worked at the steam table, approached the students and tried to warn them away. "You're acting stupid, ignorant!" she said. They didn't move. Around five-thirty, the front doors to the store were locked. The four still didn't move. Finally, they left by a side door. Outside, a small crowd had gathered, including a photographer from the Greensboro *Record*. "I'll be back tomorrow with A. & T. College," one of the students said.

By next morning, the protest had grown to twenty-seven men and four women, most from the same dormitory as the original four. The men were dressed in suits and ties. The students had brought their schoolwork, and studied as they sat at the counter. On Wednesday, students from Greensboro's "Negro" secondary school, Dudley High, joined in, and the number of protesters swelled to eighty. By Thursday, the protesters numbered three hundred, including three white women, from the Greensboro campus of the University of North Carolina. By Saturday, the sit-in had reached six hundred. People spilled out onto the street. White teen-agers waved Confederate flags. Someone threw a firecracker. At noon, the A. & T. football team arrived. "Here comes the wrecking crew," one of the white students shouted.

By the following Monday, sit-ins had spread to Winston-Salem, twenty-five miles away, and Durham, fifty miles away. The day after that, students at Fayetteville State Teachers College and at Johnson C. Smith College, in Charlotte, joined in, followed on Wednesday by students at St. Augustine's College and Shaw University, in Raleigh. On Thursday and Friday, the protest crossed state lines, surfacing in Hampton and Portsmouth, Virginia, in Rock Hill, South Carolina, and in Chattanooga, Tennessee. By the end of the month, there were sit-ins throughout the South, as far west as Texas. "I asked every student I met what the first day of the sitdowns had been like on his campus," the political theorist Michael Walzer wrote in *Dissent*. "The answer was always the same: 'It was like a fever. Everyone wanted to go.'" Some seventy thousand students eventually took part. Thousands were arrested and untold thousands more radicalized. These events in the early sixties became a civil-rights war that engulfed the South for the rest of the decade—and it happened without e-mail, texting, Facebook, or Twitter.

The world, we are told, is in the midst of a revolution. The new tools of social media have reinvented social activism. With Facebook and Twitter and the like, the traditional relationship between political authority and popular will has been upended, making it easier for the powerless to collaborate, coördinate, and give voice to their concerns. When ten thousand protesters took to the streets in Moldova in the spring of 2009 to protest against their country's Communist government, the action was dubbed the Twitter Revolution, because of the means by which the demonstrators had been brought together. A few months after that, when student protests rocked Tehran, the State Department took the unusual step of asking Twitter to suspend scheduled maintenance of its Web site, because the Administration didn't want such a critical organizing tool out of service at the height of the demonstrations. "Without Twitter the people of Iran would not have felt empowered and confident to stand up for freedom and democracy," Mark Pfeifle, a former national-security adviser, later wrote, calling for Twitter to be nominated for the Nobel Peace Prize. Where activists were once defined by their causes, they are now defined by their tools. Facebook warriors go online to push for change. "You are the best hope for us all," James K. Glassman, a former senior State Department official, told a crowd of cyber activists at a recent conference sponsored by Facebook, A. T. & T., Howcast, MTV, and Google. Sites like Facebook, Glassman said, "give the U.S. a significant competitive advantage over terrorists. Some time ago, I said that Al Qaeda was 'eating our lunch on the Internet.' That is no longer the case. Al Qaeda is stuck in Web 1.0. The Internet is now about interactivity and conversation."

These are strong, and puzzling, claims. Why does it matter who is eating whose lunch on the Internet? Are people who log on to their Facebook page really the best hope for us all? As for Moldova's so-called Twitter Revolution, Evgeny Morozov, a scholar at Stanford who has been the most persistent of digital evangelism's critics, points out that Twitter had scant internal significance in Moldova, a country where very few Twitter accounts exist. Nor does it seem to have been a revolution, not least because the protests—as Anne Applebaum suggested in the *Washington Post*—may well have been a bit of stagecraft cooked up by the government. (In a country paranoid about Romanian revanchism, the protesters flew a Romanian flag over the Parliament building.) In the Iranian case, meanwhile, the people tweeting about the demonstrations were almost all in the West. "It is time to get Twitter's role in the events in Iran right," Golnaz Esfandiari wrote, this past summer, in *Foreign Policy*. "Simply put: There was no Twitter Revolution inside Iran." The cadre of prominent bloggers, like Andrew Sullivan, who championed the role of social media in Iran, Esfandiari continued, misunderstood the situation. "Western journalists who couldn't reach—or didn't bother reaching?—people on the ground in Iran simply scrolled through the English-language tweets post with tag #iranelection," she wrote. "Through it all, no one seemed to wonder why people trying to coordinate protests in Iran would be writing in any language other than Farsi."

Some of this grandiosity is to be expected. Innovators tend to be solipsists. They often want to cram every stray fact and experience into their new model. As the historian Robert Darnton has written, "The marvels of communication technology in the present have produced a false consciousness about the past—even a sense that communication has no history, or had nothing of importance to consider before the days of television and the Internet." But there is something else at work here, in the outsized enthusiasm for social media. Fifty years after one of the most extraordinary episodes of social upheaval in American history, we seem to have forgotten what activism is.

In the Iranian case . . . the people tweeting about the demonstrations were almost all in the West.

Greensboro in the early nineteen-sixties was the kind of place where racial insubordination was routinely met with violence. The four students who first sat down at the lunch counter were terrified. "I suppose if anyone had come up behind me and yelled 'Boo,' I think I would have fallen off my seat," one of them said later. On the first day, the store man-

ager notified the police chief, who immediately sent two officers to the store. On the third day, a gang of white toughs
showed up at the lunch counter and stood ostentatiously behind the protesters, ominously muttering epithets such as
"burr-head nigger." A local Ku Klux Klan leader made an ap-
pearance. On Saturday, as tensions grew, someone called in a
bomb threat, and the entire store had to be evacuated.

The dangers were even clearer in the Mississippi Freedom
Summer Project of 1964, another of the sentinel campaigns of
the civil-rights movement. The Student Nonviolent Coordi-
nating Committee recruited hundreds of Northern, largely
white unpaid volunteers to run Freedom Schools, register
black voters, and raise civil-rights awareness in the Deep
South. "No one should go *anywhere* alone, but certainly not in
an automobile and certainly not at night," they were in-
structed. Within days of arriving in Mississippi, three volunteers—Michael Schwerner, James Chaney, and Andrew Good-
man—were kidnapped and killed, and, during the rest of the
summer, thirty-seven black churches were set on fire and dozens of safe houses were bombed; volunteers were beaten, shot
at, arrested, and trailed by pickup trucks full of armed men. A
quarter of those in the program dropped out. Activism that
challenges the status quo—that attacks deeply rooted problems—is not for the faint of heart.

What makes people capable of this kind of activism? The
Stanford sociologist Doug McAdam compared the Freedom
Summer dropouts with the participants who stayed, and discovered that the key difference wasn't, as might be expected,
ideological fervor. "*All* of the applicants—participants and
withdrawals alike—emerge as highly committed, articulate
supporters of the goals and values of the summer program,"
he concluded. What mattered more was an applicant's degree
of personal connection to the civil-rights movement. All the
volunteers were required to provide a list of personal contacts—the people they wanted kept apprised of their activi-

ties—and participants were far more likely than dropouts to have close friends who were also going to Mississippi. High-risk activism, McAdam concluded, is a "strong-tie" phenomenon.

This pattern shows up again and again. One study of the Red Brigades, the Italian terrorist group of the nineteen-seventies, found that seventy per cent of recruits had at least one good friend already in the organization. The same is true of the men who joined the mujahideen in Afghanistan. Even revolutionary actions that look spontaneous, like the demonstrations in East Germany that led to the fall of the Berlin Wall, are, at core, strong-tie phenomena. The opposition movement in East Germany consisted of several hundred groups, each with roughly a dozen members. Each group was in limited contact with the others: at the time, only thirteen per cent of East Germans even had a phone. All they knew was that on Monday nights, outside St. Nicholas Church in downtown Leipzig, people gathered to voice their anger at the state. And the primary determinant of who showed up was "critical friends"—the more friends you had who were critical of the regime the more likely you were to join the protest.

So one crucial fact about the four freshmen at the Greensboro lunch counter—David Richmond, Franklin McCain, Ezell Blair, and Joseph McNeil—was their relationship with one another. McNeil was a roommate of Blair's in A. & T.'s Scott Hall dormitory. Richmond roomed with McCain one floor up, and Blair, Richmond, and McCain had all gone to Dudley High School. The four would smuggle beer into the dorm and talk late into the night in Blair and McNeil's room. They would all have remembered the murder of Emmett Till in 1955, the Montgomery bus boycott that same year, and the showdown in Little Rock in 1957. It was McNeil who brought up the idea of a sit-in at Woolworth's. They'd discussed it for nearly a month. Then McNeil came into the dorm room and asked the others if they were ready. There was a pause, and McCain said, in a way that works only with people who talk late into the night with one another, "Are you guys chicken or not?" Ezell Blair worked up the courage the next day to ask for a cup of coffee because he was flanked by his roommate and two good friends from high school.

The kind of activism associated with social media isn't like this at all. The platforms of social media are built around weak ties. Twitter is a way of following (or being followed by) people you may never have met. Facebook is a tool for efficiently managing your acquaintances, for keeping up with the people you would not otherwise be able to stay in touch with. That's why you can have a thousand "friends" on Facebook, as you never could in real life.

This is in many ways a wonderful thing. There is strength in weak ties, as the sociologist Mark Granovetter has observed. Our acquaintances—not our friends—are our greatest source of new ideas and information. The Internet lets us exploit the power of these kinds of distant connections with marvellous efficiency. It's terrific at the diffusion of innovation, interdisciplinary collaboration, seamlessly matching up buyers and sellers, and the logistical functions of the dating world. But weak ties seldom lead to high-risk activism.

In a new book called "The Dragonfly Effect: Quick, Effective, and Powerful Ways to Use Social Media to Drive Social Change," the business consultant Andy Smith and the Stanford Business School professor Jennifer Aaker tell the story of Sameer Bhatia, a young Silicon Valley entrepreneur who came down with acute myelogenous leukemia. It's a perfect illustration of social media's strengths. Bhatia needed a bone-marrow transplant, but he could not find a match among his relatives and friends. The odds were best with a donor of his ethnicity, and there were few South Asians in the national bone-marrow database. So Bhatia's business partner sent out an e-mail explaining Bhatia's plight to more than four hundred of their acquaintances, who forwarded the e-mail to their personal contacts; Facebook pages and YouTube videos were devoted to the Help Sameer campaign. Eventually, nearly twenty-five thousand new people were registered in the bone-marrow database, and Bhatia found a match.

But how did the campaign get so many people to sign up? By not asking too much of them. That's the only way you can get someone you don't really know to do something on your behalf. You can get thousands of people to sign up for a donor registry, because doing so is pretty easy. You have to send in a cheek swab and—in the highly unlikely event that your bone marrow is a good match for someone in need—spend a few hours at the hospital. Donating bone marrow isn't a trivial matter. But it doesn't involve financial or personal risk; it doesn't mean spending a summer being chased by armed men in pickup trucks. It doesn't require that you confront socially entrenched norms and practices. In fact, it's the kind of commitment that will bring only social acknowledgment and praise.

The kind of activism associated with social media isn't like this at all. The platforms of social media are built around weak ties.

The evangelists of social media don't understand this distinction; they seem to believe that a Facebook friend is the same as a real friend and that signing up for a donor registry in Silicon Valley today is activism in the same sense as sitting at a segregated lunch counter in Greensboro in 1960. "Social networks are particularly effective at increasing motivation," Aaker and Smith write. But that's not true. Social networks are effective at increasing *participation*—by lessening the level of motivation that participation requires. The Facebook page of the Save Darfur Coalition has 1,282,339 members, who have donated an average of nine cents apiece. The next biggest Darfur charity on Facebook has 22,073 members, who have donated an average of thirty-five cents. Help Save Darfur has 2,797 members, who have given, on average, fifteen cents. A spokesperson for the Save Darfur Coalition told *Newsweek*, "We wouldn't necessarily gauge someone's value to the advocacy movement based on what they've given. This is a powerful mechanism to engage this critical population. They inform their community, attend events, volunteer. It's not something you can measure by looking at a ledger." In other words, Facebook activism succeeds not by motivating people to make a real sacrifice but by motivating them to do the things that people do when they are not motivated enough to make a real sacrifice. We are a long way from the lunch counters of Greensboro.

The students who joined the sit-ins across the South during the winter of 1960 described the movement as a "fever." But the civil-rights movement was more like a military campaign than like a contagion. In the late nineteen-fifties, there had been sixteen sit-ins in various cities throughout the South, fifteen of which were formally organized by civil-rights organizations like the N.A.A.C.P. and CORE. Possible locations for activism were scouted. Plans were drawn up. Movement activists held training sessions and retreats for would-be protesters. The Greensboro Four were a product of this groundwork: all were members of the N.A.A.C.P. Youth Council. They had close ties with the head of the local N.A.A.C.P. chapter. They had been briefed on the earlier wave of sit-ins in Durham, and had been part of a series of movement meetings in activist churches. When the sit-in movement spread from Greensboro throughout the South, it did not spread indiscriminately. It spread to those cities which had preexisting "movement centers"—a core of dedicated and trained activists ready to turn the "fever" into action.

The civil-rights movement was high-risk activism. It was also, crucially, strategic activism: a challenge to the establishment mounted with precision and discipline. The N.A.A.C.P.

was a centralized organization, run from New York according to highly formalized operating procedures. At the Southern Christian Leadership Conference, Martin Luther King, Jr., was the unquestioned authority. At the center of the movement was the black church, which had, as Aldon D. Morris points out in his superb 1984 study, "The Origins of the Civil Rights Movement," a carefully demarcated division of labor, with various standing committees and disciplined groups. "Each group was task-oriented and coordinated its activities through authority structures," Morris writes. "Individuals were held accountable for their assigned duties, and important conflicts were resolved by the minister, who usually exercised ultimate authority over the congregation."

This is the second crucial distinction between traditional activism and its online variant: social media are not about this kind of hierarchical organization. Facebook and the like are tools for building *networks*, which are the opposite, in structure and character, of hierarchies. Unlike hierarchies, with their rules and procedures, networks aren't controlled by a single central authority. Decisions are made through consensus, and the ties that bind people to the group are loose.

This structure makes networks enormously resilient and adaptable in low-risk situations. Wikipedia is a perfect example. It doesn't have an editor, sitting in New York, who directs and corrects each entry. The effort of putting together each entry is self-organized. If every entry in Wikipedia were to be erased tomorrow, the content would swiftly be restored, because that's what happens when a network of thousands spontaneously devote their time to a task.

There are many things, though, that networks don't do well. Car companies sensibly use a network to organize their hundreds of suppliers, but not to design their cars. No one believes that the articulation of a coherent design philosophy is best handled by a sprawling, leaderless organizational system. Because networks don't have a centralized leadership structure and clear lines of authority, they have real difficulty reaching consensus and setting goals. They can't think strategically; they are chronically prone to conflict and error. How do you make difficult choices about tactics or strategy or philosophical direction when everyone has an equal say?

The second crucial distinction between traditional activism and its online variant [is that] . . . social media are not about . . . hierarchical organization.

The Palestine Liberation Organization originated as a network, and the international-relations scholars Mette Eilstrup-Sangiovanni and Calvert Jones argue in a recent essay in *International Security* that this is why it ran into such trouble as it grew: "Structural features typical of networks—the absence of central authority, the unchecked autonomy of rival groups, and the inability to arbitrate quarrels through formal mechanisms—made the P.L.O. excessively vulnerable to outside manipulation and internal strife."

In Germany in the nineteen-seventies, they go on, "the far more unified and successful left-wing terrorists tended to organize hierarchically, with professional management and clear divisions of labor. They were concentrated geographically in universities, where they could establish central leadership, trust, and camaraderie through regular, face-to-face meetings." They seldom betrayed their comrades in arms during police interrogations. Their counterparts on the right were organized as decentralized networks, and had no such discipline. These groups were regularly infiltrated, and members, once arrested, easily gave up their comrades. Similarly, Al Qaeda was most dangerous when it was a unified hierarchy. Now that it has dissipated into a network, it has proved far less effective.

The drawbacks of networks scarcely matter if the network isn't interested in systemic change—if it just wants to frighten or humiliate or make a splash—or if it doesn't need to think strategically. But if you're taking on a powerful and organized establishment you have to be a hierarchy. The Montgomery bus boycott required the participation of tens of thousands of people who depended on public transit to get to and from work each day. It lasted a *year*. In order to persuade those people to stay true to the cause, the boycott's organizers tasked each local black church with maintaining morale, and put together a free alternative private carpool service, with forty-eight dispatchers and forty-two pickup stations. Even the White Citizens Council, King later said, conceded that the carpool system moved with "military precision." By the time King came to Birmingham, for the climactic showdown with Police Commissioner Eugene (Bull) Connor, he had a budget of a million dollars, and a hundred full-time staff members on the ground, divided into operational units. The operation itself was divided into steadily escalating phases, mapped out in advance. Support was maintained through consecutive mass meetings rotating from church to church around the city.

Boycotts and sit-ins and nonviolent confrontations—which were the weapons of choice for the civil-rights movement—are high-risk strategies. They leave little room for conflict and error. The moment even one protester deviates from the script and responds to provocation, the moral legitimacy of the entire protest is compromised. Enthusiasts for social media would no doubt have us believe that King's task in Birmingham would have been made infinitely easier had he been able to communicate with his followers through Facebook, and contented himself with tweets from a Birmingham jail. But networks are messy: think of the ceaseless pattern of correction and revision, amendment and debate, that characterizes Wikipedia. If Martin Luther King, Jr., had tried to do a wiki-boycott in Montgomery, he would have been steamrollered by the white power structure. And of what use would a digital communication tool be in a town where ninety-eight per cent of the black community could be reached every Sunday morning at church? The things that King needed in Birmingham—discipline and strategy—were things that online social media cannot provide.

The bible of the social-media movement is Clay Shirky's "Here Comes Everybody." Shirky, who teaches at New York University, sets out to demonstrate the organizing power of the Internet, and he begins with the story of Evan, who worked on Wall Street, and his friend Ivanna, after she left her smart phone, an expensive Sidekick, on the back seat of a New York City taxicab. The telephone company transferred the data on Ivanna's lost phone to a new phone, whereupon she and Evan discovered that the Sidekick was now in the hands of a teenager from Queens, who was using it to take photographs of herself and her friends.

When Evan e-mailed the teenager, Sasha, asking for the phone back, she replied that his "white ass" didn't deserve to have it back. Miffed, he set up a Web page with her picture and a description of what had happened. He forwarded the link to his friends, and they forwarded it to their friends. Someone found the MySpace page of Sasha's boyfriend, and a link to it found its way onto the site. Someone found her address online and took a video of her home while driving by; Evan posted the video on the site. The story was picked up by the news filter Digg. Evan was now up to ten e-mails a minute. He created a bulletin board for his readers to share their stories, but it crashed under the weight of responses. Evan and Ivanna went to the police, but the police filed the report under "lost," rather than "stolen," which essentially closed the case. "By this point millions of readers were watching," Shirky writes, "and dozens of mainstream news outlets had covered the story." Bowing to the pressure, the N.Y.P.D. reclassified the item as "stolen." Sasha was arrested, and Evan got his friend's Sidekick back.

Shirky's argument is that this is the kind of thing that could never have happened in the pre-Internet age—and he's right. Evan could never have tracked down Sasha. The story of the Sidekick would never have been publicized. An army of people could never have been assembled to wage this fight. The police wouldn't have bowed to the pressure of a lone person who had misplaced something as trivial as a cell phone. The story, to Shirky, illustrates "the ease and speed with which a group can be mobilized for the right kind of cause" in the Internet age.

Shirky considers this model of activism an upgrade. But it is simply a form of organizing which favors the weak-tie connections that give us access to information over the strong-tie connections that help us persevere in the face of danger. It shifts our energies from organizations that promote strategic and disciplined activity and toward those which promote resilience and adaptability. It makes it easier for activists to express themselves, and harder for that expression to have any impact. The instruments of social media are well suited to making the existing social order more efficient. They are not a natural enemy of the status quo. If you are of the opinion that all the world needs is a little buffing around the edges, this should not trouble you. But if you think that there are still lunch counters out there that need integrating it ought to give you pause.

Shirky ends the story of the lost Sidekick by asking, portentously, "What happens next?"—no doubt imagining future waves of digital protesters. But he has already answered the question. What happens next is more of the same. A networked, weak-tie world is good at things like helping Wall Streeters get phones back from teen-age girls. *Viva la revolución.*

Revolutions Can Still Be Repressed by Brutal Military Force Even in the Digital Age

Peter Osnos

Peter Osnos, a former correspondent for the Washington Post *newspaper, is the founder and editor-at-large of PublicAffairs books.*

In early March [2011], I attended a roundtable at the Paley Center for Media called "The Fourth Estate in a Digital Democracy." On reflection only a few weeks later, that gathering and the countless others like it celebrating the prominence of social media have been given a chastening lesson. The centerpiece of the discussion was the role of Facebook and Twitter in the unfolding revolutions in Tunisia, Egypt, and, in its early days then, Libya, with ripples elsewhere in North Africa and the Middle East. The essence of the issue came down to the positions of two media celebrities who were not actually present but had this exchange in the current *Foreign Affairs*: "Even the increased sophistication and force of state reaction," wrote Clay Shirky, "underline the basic point: these tools alter the dynamics of the public sphere. Where the state prevails, it is only reacting to citizens' ability to be more publicly vocal and to coordinate more rapidly and on a larger scale than before these tools existed."

Malcolm Gladwell's response was that, for Shirky's "argument to be anything close to persuasive, (he) has to convince readers that in the absence of social media, those uprisings would not have been possible."

Overwhelming Technology

Two major developments have now demonstrated how abruptly what seems like certainties about technology and communications can be overwhelmed. In Libya, Muammar Gaddafi's brutal counterattack transformed the initial successes of opposition groups into a massive retreat. Finally, the United Nations Security Council and the Arab League authorized a military response now unfolding. But as Gaddafi routed his opponents, little more was said about Facebook and Twitter. And then there is the cataclysm in Japan. One of the world's most advanced societies has been devastated by the power of nature. For all the technology available to the Japanese, the country has been at the mercy of what has turned out to be a cascade of catastrophes that no amount of 140 character messages and updates to friends could handle, as communications of all kinds were disabled across stricken areas and even, at times, in Tokyo.

It is pointless to dispute that digital advances have played an enormous role in recent years in the speed of communications, and, in some situations, Egypt and Tunisia certainly among them, these technologies have played a meaningful part in the rallying of crowds and in garnering international recognition. A global generation of mainly young people will continue to refine and use the capacity to reach out to each other. Turmoil reflects the conditions of the era in which it occurs, and social media are very much a factor of our age.

As [Libyan dictator Muammar] Gaddafi routed his opponents, little more was said about Facebook and Twitter.

But as I listened to the Paley Center dialogue, I recalled two transformations in the latter years of the twentieth century that proved revolution has a dynamic that transcends contemporary gadgetry. These were indigenous revolutions, that of course had their origins in widespread discontent, but they were led by charismatic religious figures around whom people mobilized, for better and for worse.

Both examples took place in 1979, when I was the foreign editor of the *Washington Post*. The surprise choice of Polish Cardinal Karol Wojtyla as Pope John Paul II and his trip soon thereafter to his homeland was unquestionably a trigger in what culminated a decade later in the fall of Communism throughout the Eastern Bloc and eventually the Soviet Union. I was in Poland for those ten amazing days in June and watched as crowds in the millions gathered wherever the Pope was scheduled to appear. If there was any institution responsible for the celebration, it was the Church. But in reality, Poles had found a way to express themselves that confounded the oppressive regime that ruled them. These were not specifically political demonstrations, but in retrospect the Polish leaders and their Kremlin overseers realized that the Pope had unleashed a measure of self-confidence that proved to be a power greater than the police state. There were setbacks to follow: martial law was imposed in 1981 to forestall a Soviet invasion. But from the moment the Pope arrived in Warsaw in 1979, Communism was in its final period.

No matter how vividly the repression is . . . described on Facebook and Twitter, reform in Iran has been brutally stifled.

Also in 1979 came the Iranian revolution, which ousted the Shah, who like the autocratic leaders in Egypt and Tunisia, had seemed supremely in charge until, suddenly he wasn't. It was the Ayatollah Khomeini from his exile in Paris whose fervent perorations circulated in cassettes galvanized the population and turned the country in a matter of months from a relatively progressive society, at least in social norms, to what it has become: a country run by Mullahs with the capacity and will to crush opposition and cling to power. No matter how vividly the repression is displayed in cellphone camera footage on YouTube or described on Facebook and Twitter, reform in Iran has been brutally stifled. The regime has even turned social media against its own people by tracking their use of it and arresting or intimidating those identified.

Religious expression as ancient as the teachings of Jesus Christ in Poland and Mohammad in Iran were the underpinnings of revolution in those two nations. If there is a broader message in the events of this past month, it is how abruptly change (even in the digital age) can be swept aside by the deployment of unrelenting military force against the will of the people or the force of nature at its fiercest, a tectonic shift on a massive scale. As we recognize the influence of all that is new in our times, we should also be humbled by these reminders of eternal powers.

Authoritarian Regimes Can Use the Internet to Their Advantage

The Economist

The Economist *is a British weekly newspaper focusing on international politics and business news and opinion.*

When thousands of young Iranians took to the streets in June 2009 to protest against the apparent rigging of the presidential election, much of the coverage in the Western media focused on the protesters' use of Twitter, a microblogging service. "This would not happen without Twitter," declared the *Wall Street Journal.* Andrew Sullivan, a prominent American-based blogger, also proclaimed Twitter to be "the critical tool for organising the resistance in Iran". The *New York Times* said the demonstrations pitted "thugs firing bullets" against "protesters firing tweets".

The idea that the internet was fomenting revolution and promoting democracy in Iran was just the latest example of the widely held belief that communications technology, and the internet in particular, is inherently pro-democratic. In this gleefully iconoclastic book [*The Net Delusion: The Dark Side of Internet Freedom*], Evgeny Morozov takes a stand against this "cyber-utopian" view, arguing that the internet can be just as effective at sustaining authoritarian regimes. By assuming that the internet is always pro-democratic, he says, Western policymakers are operating with a "voluntary intellectual handicap" that makes it harder rather than easier to promote democracy.

He starts with the events in Iran, which illustrate his argument in microcosm. An investigation by Al Jazeera, an international news network based in Qatar, could confirm only 60 active Twitter accounts in Tehran. Iranian bloggers who took part in the protests have since poured cold water on the "Twitter revolution" theory. But the American government's endorsement of the theory, together with the State Department's request that Twitter delay some planned maintenance that would have taken the service offline for a few crucial hours at the height of the unrest, prompted the Iranian authorities to crack down on social networks of all kinds. Iranians entering the country were, for example, looked up on Facebook to see if they had links to any known dissidents, thus achieving the very opposite of what American policymakers wanted.

Authoritarian regimes can use the internet, as well as greater access to other kinds of media, such as television, to their advantage.

The root of the problem, Mr Morozov argues, is that Western policymakers see an all-too-neat parallel with the role that radio propaganda and photocopiers may have played in undermining the Soviet Union. A native of Belarus, Mr Morozov (who has occasionally written for *The Economist*) says this oversimplification of history has led to the erroneous conclusion that promoting internet access and "internet freedom" will have a similar effect on authoritarian regimes today.

In fact, authoritarian regimes can use the internet, as well as greater access to other kinds of media, such as television, to their advantage. Allowing East Germans to watch American soap operas on West German television, for example, seems to have acted as a form of pacification that actually reduced people's interest in politics. Surveys found that East Germans with access to Western television were less likely to express dissatisfaction with the regime. As one East German dissident lamented, "the whole people could leave the country and move to the West as a man at 8pm, via television."

Mr Morozov catalogues many similar examples of the internet being used with similarly pacifying consequences today, as authoritarian regimes make an implicit deal with their populations: help yourselves to pirated films, silly video clips and online pornography, but stay away from politics. "The internet", Mr Morozov argues, "has provided so many cheap and easily available entertainment fixes to those living under authoritarianism that it has become considerably harder to get people to care about politics at all."

Social networks offer a cheaper and easier way to identify dissidents than other, more traditional forms of surveillance. Despite talk of a "dictator's dilemma", censorship technology is sophisticated enough to block politically sensitive material without impeding economic activity, as China's example shows. The internet can be used to spread propaganda very effectively, which is why Hugo Chávez is on Twitter. The web can also be effective in supporting the government line, or at least casting doubt on critics' position (China has an army of pro-government bloggers). Indeed, under regimes where nobody believes the official media, pro-government propaganda spread via the internet is actually perceived by many to be more credible by comparison.

Authoritarian governments are assumed to be clueless about the internet, but they often understand its political uses far better than their Western counterparts do, Mr Morozov suggests. His profiles in "The Net Delusion" of the Russian government's young internet advisers are particularly illuminating. Previous technologies, including the telegraph, aircraft, radio and television, were also expected to bolster democracy, he observes, but they failed to live up to expectations. The proliferation of channels means that Americans watch less TV news than they did in the pre-cable era. And by endorsing Twitter, Facebook and Google as pro-democratic instruments, the American government has compromised their neutrality and encouraged authoritarian regimes to regard them as agents of its foreign policy.

So what does Mr Morozov propose instead of the current approach? He calls for "cyber-realism" to replace "cyber-utopianism", making it clear that he believes that technology can indeed be used to promote democracy, provided it is done in the right way. But he presents little in the way of specific prescriptions, other than to stress the importance of considering the social and political context in which technology is deployed, rather than focusing on the characteristics of the technology itself, as internet gurus tend to. Every authoritarian regime is different, he argues, so it is implausible that the same approach will work in each case; detailed local knowledge is vital. Yet having done such a good job of knocking down his opponents' arguments, it is a pity he does not have more concrete proposals to offer in their place.

Social networks offer a cheaper and easier way to identify dissidents than other, more traditional forms of surveillance.

With chapter titles and headings such as "Why the KGB wants you to join Facebook" and "Why Kierkegaard Hates Slacktivism" it is clear that Mr Morozov is enjoying himself (indeed, there may be a few more bad jokes than is strictly necessary). But the resulting book is not just unfailingly readable: it is also a provocative, enlightening and welcome riposte to the cyber-utopian worldview.

CHAPTER 4

How Will the Media's Role in Politics Evolve in Coming Years?

Chapter Overview

Tom Rosenstiel and Amy Mitchell

Tom Rosenstiel is an author, journalist, press critic, and founder and director of the Pew Research Center's Project for Excellence in Journalism, a nonpolitical, nonpartisan research institute. Amy Mitchell is deputy director of the Project.

By several measures, the state of the American news media improved in 2010.

After two dreadful years, most sectors of the industry saw revenue begin to recover. With some notable exceptions, cutbacks in newsrooms eased. And while still more talk than action some experiments with new revenue models began to show signs of blossoming.

A Challenge to Journalism

Among the major sectors, only newspapers suffered continued revenue declines last year—an unmistakable sign that the structural economic problems facing newspapers are more severe than those of other media. When the final tallies are in, we estimate 1,000 to 1,500 more newsroom jobs will have been lost—meaning newspaper newsrooms are 30% smaller than in 2000.

Beneath all this, however, a more fundamental challenge to journalism became clearer in the last year. The biggest issue ahead may not be lack of audience or even lack of new revenue experiments. It may be that in the digital realm the news industry is no longer in control of its own future.

News organizations—old and new—still produce most of the content audiences consume. But each technological advance has added a new layer of complexity—and a new set of players—in connecting that content to consumers and advertisers.

In the digital space, the organizations that produce the news increasingly rely on independent networks to sell their ads. They depend on aggregators (such as Google) and social networks (such as Facebook) to bring them a substantial portion of their audience. And now, as news consumption becomes more mobile, news companies must follow the rules of device makers (such as Apple) and software developers (Google again) to deliver their content. Each new platform often requires a new software program. And the new players take a share of the revenue and in many cases also control the audience data.

The migration to the web ... continued to gather speed.
In 2010 every news platform saw audiences either stall
or decline—except for the web.

That data may be the most important commodity of all. In a media world where consumers decide what news they want to get and how they want to get it, the future will belong to those who understand the public's changing behavior and can target content and advertising to snugly fit the interests of each user. That knowledge—and the expertise in gathering it—increasingly resides with technology companies outside journalism.

In the 20th century, the news media thrived by being the intermediary others needed to reach customers. In the 21st, increasingly there is a new intermediary: Software programmers, content aggregators and device makers control access to the public. The news industry, late to adapt and culturally more tied to content creation than engineering, finds itself more a follower than leader shaping its business.

Migration to the Web

Meanwhile, the pace of change continues to accelerate. Mobile has already become an important factor in news. A new survey released with this year's report, produced with Pew Internet and American Life Project in association with the Knight Foundation, finds that nearly half of all Americans (47%) now get some form of local news on a mobile device. What they turn to most there is news that serves immediate needs—weather, information about restaurants and other local businesses, and traffic. And the move to mobile is only likely to grow. By January 2011, 7% of Americans reported owning some kind of electronic tablet. That was nearly double the number just four months earlier.

The migration to the web also continued to gather speed. In 2010 every news platform saw audiences either stall or decline—except for the web. Cable news, one of the growth sectors of the last decade, is now shrinking, too. For the first time in at least a dozen years, the median audience declined at all three cable news channels.

For the first time, too, more people said they got news from the web than newspapers. The internet now trails only television among American adults as a destination for news, and the trend line shows the gap closing. Financially the tipping point also has come. When the final tally is in, online ad revenue in 2010 is projected to surpass print newspaper ad revenue for the first time. The problem for news is that by far the largest share of that online ad revenue goes to non-news sources, particularly to aggregators.

In the past, much of the experimentation in new journalism occurred locally, often financed by charitable grants, usually at small scale. Larger national online-only news organizations focused more on aggregation than original reporting. In 2010, however, some of the biggest new media institutions began to develop original newsgathering in a significant way. Yahoo added several dozen reporters across news, sports and finance. AOL had 900 journalists, 500 of them at its local Patch news operation (it then let go 200 people from the content team after the merger with Huffingtonpost). By the end of 2011, Bloomberg expects to have 150 journalists and analysts for its new Washington operation, Bloomberg Government. News Corp. has hired from 100 or 150, depending on the press reports, for its new tablet newspaper, *The Daily*, though not all may be journalists. Together these hires come close to matching the jobs in 2010 we estimate were lost in newspapers, the first time we have seen this kind of substitution.

A report in this year's study also finds that new community media sites are beginning to put as much energy into securing new revenue streams—and refining audiences to do so—as creating content. Many also say they are doing more to curate user content.

With lower pay, more demands for speed, less training, and more volunteer work, there is a general devaluing and even . . . a "de-skilling" of the profession [of journalism].

Trouble for Traditional News and Journalism

Traditional newsrooms, meanwhile, are different places than they were before the recession. They are smaller, their aspirations have narrowed and their journalists are stretched thinner. But their leaders also say they are more adaptive, younger and more engaged in multimedia presentation, aggregation, blogging and user content. In some ways, new media and old, slowly and sometimes grudgingly, are coming to resemble each other.

The result is a news ecology full of experimentation and excitement, but also one that is uneven, has uncertain financial underpinning and some clear holes in coverage. Even in

Seattle, one of the most vibrant places for new media, "some vitally important stories are less likely to be covered," said Diane Douglas who runs a local civic group and considers the decentralization of media voices a healthy change. "It's very frightening to think of those gaps and all the more insidious because you don't know what you don't know." Some also worry that with lower pay, more demands for speed, less training, and more volunteer work, there is a general devaluing and even what scholar Robert Picard has called a "de-skilling" of the profession.

Traditional Media Are Losing Out to Social Media as a Source for Political Information

Katie Kindelan

Katie Kindelan is a writer who resides in the Washington, DC, area and contributes frequently to the online magazine Social Times.

Americans trust social media more than traditional news outlets, and Republicans and Tea Party supporters have caught up with Democrats in embracing social media, a new study shows.

Voters Rely on Social Networking Sites

The latest study of social media and politics from the Pew Research Center found that 53 percent of voters said they used social networking sites like Twitter and Facebook to follow politics because they felt the information was more reliable than what they received through traditional news media.

58 percent of respondents identifying themselves as Democratic voters said they use social media, compared with 54 percent of Republicans. Compare that to 2008, when 44 percent of Democrats identified themselves as social networkers compared to 29 percent of Republicans.

In short, researchers found that while Democrats made the most use of social media in the 2008 election, Republicans virtually erased the gap in 2010.

Among overall social network users, 40 percent of Republican voters and 38 percent of Democratic voters used those sites to become involved politically. Among those using social media to specifically follow politics, 45 percent said they voted Republican versus 41 percent for Democrats.

> *53 percent of voters said they used social networking sites ... to follow politics because they felt the information was more reliable than what they received through traditional news media.*

In all, Pew found 21 percent of adult Internet users said they used social networking sites, from Facebook to Twitter and MySpace, to find out who their friends were voting for, get candidate information, post comments, 'friend' candidates and campaigns, and take part in group causes.

Much of the Republican growth, researchers concluded, can be attributed to the normal trajectory of technological advancements. In 2008, sites like Facebook and Twitter were new and the Obama campaign adopted them early. Now everybody is on a social network, and adept at the latest technologies.

"Everybody learned from the Obama campaign in 2008 that social media can be an effective tool to contact and galvanize voters," said Lee Rainie, the study's lead researcher and director of the Pew Internet & American Life Project.

In 2008, Obama had a 15-point advantage over his opponent, Republican John McCain, with adults who use social media.

Adults Quickly Adapting to Social Media

Younger Internet users, Pew found, remain more likely to use social media for political activities, but people over age 50 are the fastest-growing demographic group using social media, according to Pew, another harbinger for the Republican gains.

In 2010, 33 percent of social media users over the age of 50 said they used social networking sites for politics, compared to 42 percent of those under the age of 30.

In this election, supporters of the Tea Party movement also proved especially active on social media sites, with 23 percent saying they used the sites to get candidate or campaign information, 19 percent saying they posted political content on social media sites and 22 percent saying they used social media to "friend" a candidate or cause.

Younger Internet users . . . remain more likely to use social media for political activities, but people over age 50 are the fastest-growing demographic group using social media.

Overall, the study found three out of four adults are Internet users, and of them, 61 percent, use social networking sites such as Facebook or MySpace, while just 8 percent use Twitter.

The Pew study was conducted from November 3 through November 24, 2010 among 2,257 voting aged adults.

Politicians Will Increase Their Usage of Social Media in the Future

Jesse Stanchak

Jesse Stanchak is a graduate of George Washington University and editor at SmartBrief, a media company that culls and summarizes the "must-read" news in twenty-five key industries.

Each election cycle sees social media become a slightly more potent force in U.S. politics—but its effects are still relatively limited, according to panelists at an event organized by Politico and Facebook and held at the George Washington University.

A recent GWU/Politico poll found 89% of respondents said they had never directly interacted with a politician through a social network—compared with 2% who say they did once, 7% who say they do it occasionally and 2% who say they do so frequently. GWU professor Matthew Hindman noted that he expects these numbers to increase by 2012, as more young people who grew up with social technology reach voting age.

But Facebook's Adam Conner says asking about direct engagement is deceptive. Rather than asking how many people have directly engaged a candidate through a social network, Conner says it would be better to study how many people have gotten information about a candidate through their Facebook newsfeed because one of their friends supports that candidate. "That's where you get the viral feedback loops," he said.

Most campaigns are spending less than 5% of their budgets on their online efforts, said EngageDC's Mindy Finn, who served as Mitt Romney's online strategy head for his 2008 presidential campaign—though for some ballot initiative campaigns, that number can climb as high as 15%.

[The numbers of voters interacting with politicians through the Internet will] increase by 2012, as more young people who grew up with social technology reach voting age.

Part of the problem is that right now most social-media efforts for campaigns are just "window dressing," said Hindman. Candidates have Facebook and Twitter accounts just so they can say they have them—not so that they can accomplish any specific goals with them.

That could change, however, as more candidates who are personally comfortable with social tools run for office, noted Finn and Conner. Finn pointed to Gov. Rick Perry of Texas, who has a personal Twitter account, but also has an official campaign account run by staff. This allows Perry to have an authentic voice on the network. At the same time, his staff members have a channel for pushing out their updates in a transparent way.

How will the intersection of social media and politics change between now and the next cycle? The panelists offered several predictions:

Shifting focus: The goal of a campaign's online presence has shifted significantly during the past 10 years, the panelists noted. Prior to the 2004 election cycle, candidates were using their online presences to try to push out information in a way that would persuade undecided voters. Howard Dean's run for the Democratic president nomination in 2004 changed all that and made a campaign's online efforts all about firing up the base, said Hindman. The panelists posited that perhaps in the future there will be another shift, as campaigns look to engage voters.

Understanding the tools better: Finn lamented that so few candidates treat their tweets and Facebook status updates as separate platforms and understand how to appropriately use each tool. Finn says she hopes mobile engagement will be a major player in the next cycle and candidates will finally start using each platform in an appropriate fashion.

Merging video and social: Murphy Putnam Media's Philip de Vellis argued that video platforms and social media are going to converge, giving campaigns new opportunities to target and engage viewers.

Rethinking candor: Being authentic online as a candidate means taking risks, the panelists noted. And while unscripted authenticity has gone badly for some candidates, de Vellis argued that voter expectations are changing as a result. While candidates still experience the occasional "gotcha" moment, voters are beginning to become more accustomed to these gaffs—and more forgiving, he noted. As social-media mistakes become more commonplace, their cost decreases—which encourages more authenticity, he argued.

Moving beyond the campaign: Sam Arora, a candidate running for the House of Delegates in Maryland, said he used social tools to connect with voters he met while canvassing door to door, so that those initial contacts can turn into more sustained relationships. Conner mused that if Arora won his contest, he'd be able to use those online relationships to gauge how constituents felt about issues and do a better job of representing them.

Social Media Allow Political Candidates to Bypass Traditional Media

Glen Johnson

Glen Johnson is politics editor at boston.com, a news and sports website run by the Boston Globe, *the city's daily newspaper.*

Tim Pawlenty announced he was forming a presidential exploratory committee via Facebook.

President Obama announced he was seeking reelection to the highest office in the country via a YouTube video.

Mitt Romney sent out his retort via Twitter.

Collectively, those developments have highlighted the prominent role social media will play in the 2012 presidential campaign.

The days of Howard Dean putting the outline of a baseball bat on a website and asking supporters to "fill it up" with donations seems so 2004.

The same is true for the supporter text-messaging that Obama and the other candidates employed in 2008 and still use today.

This election cycle, the announced, nearly announced, and potential candidates are taking full advantage of digital media to communicate their message directly to potential supporters.

It allows them to bypass what George W. Bush used to call "the filter," and what Sarah Palin has more tartly termed "the lamestream media."

For the candidates, it's also an affordable and immediate way to spread their views.

Go back no further than that 2004 campaign to see the evolution in full.

Glen Johnson, "Social Media Let Candidates Bypass Traditional Media," boston.com, April 5, 2011. Reproduced by permission.

Massachusetts Senator John Kerry spent all of 2001 and 2002 traveling the country, building a network of financial supporters, and holding traditional rubber-chicken fundraisers as he prepared for his 2004 White House campaign.

[Social media allow political candidates] to bypass what George W. Bush used to call "the filter," and what Sarah Palin has more tartly termed "the lamestream media."

He identified activists in each city, sent them a paper invitation, reconfirmed their attendance, and then came to town, sat through a series of introductory remarks, and made his pitch himself. Then he got on a plane, flew somewhere else, and repeated the exercise.

In 2003, Dean adviser Joe Trippi and other aides got the bright idea to harness the Internet to their advantage. They put the bat or a thermometer on Dean's website, sent out an email, and urged supporters to fill it up or "raise" the temperature.

Dean broke all sorts of fundraising records with far less of the in-person networking—and travel wear-and-tear—that had been the underpinning of Kerry's campaign.

In 2008, Obama proved deft at incorporating digital media into his campaign, so much so that he installed a new media office in the White House and began simultaneously releasing his weekly radio address with an online video.

Fast-forward four years and the now-president kicked off his second campaign with a tightly choreographed video that was posted on the date and time of his choosing: before sunrise Monday.

It featured a white man, Hispanic woman, and white woman, all from swing states: North Carolina, Nevada, and Colorado, respectively.

A fourth person featured was the prototypical idealistic college student, admittedly too young to vote for the president in 2008 but eager to do so four years hence.

The final speaker was an African-American woman, a silent reminder to the 2008 Democratic coalition that they helped make Obama the country's first black president.

Even the message delivered by "Ed," the white man from North Carolina (incidentally, the state where the Democrats will hold their national nominating convention next year), included a pitch to another potent bloc: independents.

"I don't agree with Obama on everything, but I respect him and I trust him," he said.

Romney, heading from Utah to Kansas as he continues to lay the foundation for his own announcement didn't need a television or newspaper reporter to offer his response. He did it himself in fewer than 140 characters.

"@barackobama I look forward to hearing details on your jobs plan, as are 14m unemployed Americans," @MittRomney said in his cheeky post.

Pawlenty, meanwhile, showed how cognizant his campaign is of the power invested in social media.

He did Romney one better, giving his response via his own YouTube commercial.

"How can America 'Win the Future' when we're losing the present?" said Pawlenty, appropriating Obama's speech signature for his own purposes.

Then, dropping any pretense, the former governor looked directly into the camera and said, "In order for America to take a new direction, it's going to take a new president."

Last month, Pawlenty used a similar YouTube video in concert with his Facebook posting to announce his exploratory committee.

None of this is to say that there is no role for the mainstream media in the unfolding election cycle (note to self: insert sigh of relief here). The candidates themselves have affirmed its relevance.

Many of the potential GOP contenders have enriched themselves and built followings through commentary posts at the Fox News Channel.

Others, especially, Romney, have taken advantage of traditional news dissemination channels with op-ed pieces that, again, allow them to say exactly what they want to say, when they want to say it.

There are no immediate followup questions on the opinion pages.

And not for nothing, but all the candidates will count on the amplifying effects of traditional news coverage when they personally declare their candidacy.

While Obama announced his intentions Monday with a series of Internet bits and bytes that composed a video, eventually he's going to want to step in front of a live audience, with a red-white-and-blue backdrop, and ride a wave of free-media publicity with a traditional announcement.

If nothing else, it provides great crowd shots for future campaign videos.

Traditional Media Must Adapt to the Digital World or Die

Brandon Paton

Brandon Paton blogs on his website, brandonpaton.com.

The Internet has given traditional media an ultimatum: Adopt the ways of new media companies, or die a painful death.

Publishers of newspapers, magazines, and cable television (i.e. traditional media) are already struggling to survive in the world of new media. Market share of traditional media companies is consistently lost to new media counterparts. It's only a matter of time before traditional media is gone for good, leaving the best adapted companies standing.

Shifts in Consumer Expectations

On the Internet consumers expect quality information, news, and entertainment to be free, convenient, and instantly accessible. It is easy for the internet based new media companies to satisfy these expectations, while traditional media companies find it much harder.

The Internet as a platform for the distribution of media incurs a fraction of the expenses associated with traditional media. Printing, shipping, and many other expenses are largely eliminated, while most major expenses of new media are scalable. This allows new media companies to provide services and content for free by relying solely on revenue from advertisers to maintain profitability.

These consumer expectations will only be enforced as the number of households with broadband internet increases. A study by Pew Internet in April 2009 says that 63% of households have high-speed internet, up 15% from 2008.

How They'll Survive

Cable television has already begun streaming free episodes online. Websites such as Hulu.com have done a good job monetizing and consolidating shows from multiple networks into one platform. The only mistake cable networks have made is limiting the number of weeks they allow episodes to be streamed online. Scrubs, which is a show in its 8th season on ABC has only the 6 most recent episodes available online. This encourages consumers to watch episodes on illegal websites that cannot be monetized by the cable networks. By offering all episodes online with no limits, networks would have a better chance of building their audience base while monetizing a greater number of video impressions.

As print media continues to slow, companies must scale back their offline publication efforts and begin to focus on their online presence.

The majority of newspaper publications have some type of version available online. Even so, their internal infrastructure is still optimized for offline publications, which is okay as long as they are profitable in the short term. But as print media continues to slow, companies must scale back their offline publication efforts and begin to focus on their online presence. Companies who understand the evolving market and concentrate equally on online and offline publications are the companies that have the highest chance at sustainability.

One fatal mistake, similar to what has happened with online video from cable networks, is that some newspapers with simultaneous online publications are limiting access by a mandatory membership. The Internet offers countless sources of free news that are just as good as the bigger names in the industry. In order for newspapers to succeed they must exploit their name, reputation, and offline audience in order to generate momentum for their online publication, which will be their main source of long-term revenue in the future. Newspapers that restrict their content to members only, such as *The Wall Street Journal*, give potential online-only readers a reason to go elsewhere for their news.

Magazines, for the most part, are in the same situation as newspapers. Magazines are published weekly or biweekly, and simply do not satisfy consumers' expectation for instant access of recently written content. Blogs and microblogs (such as Twitter) has created a viable alternative to print magazines that offer an instantly accessible source of constantly updated information and news for free. Magazines, similarly to newspapers, should follow the model set by today's successful online-only blogs, and hope for the best.

Adapt or Die

The way in which people access media is rapidly changing, and traditional media companies can either take the risk and adapt, or keep fighting a losing battle. At this point, traditional media companies still have time to proactively adapt to the evolving marketplace. The actions taken by traditional media companies in the next couple years will determine their fate. It is survival of the fittest at its best.

The Traditional Media Will Continue to Provide Original News Content

Tom Price

Tom Price is a Washington, DC-based writer and author who focuses on public affairs, business, technology, and education. Previously he was a correspondent in the Cox Newspapers Washington bureau and chief politics writer for the Cox papers in Dayton, Ohio.

Last year [2009] was a watershed for the Internet as news source, no doubt about it. But while they are growing and becoming more significant, new-media outlets are still not filling all the gaps left by the decline of newspapers and other traditional media, according to this year's Project for Excellence in Journalism report titled "The State of the News Media."

Both Old and New Media

More than a third of Americans reported getting most of their 2008 campaign news from the Internet—three times as many as in 2004, according to a survey by the Pew Research Center for the People & the Press. For national and international affairs, only television outranked the Internet as a news source. Young voters and political activists alike turned to the Internet for news as much as they did television.

Despite the fact that the gap is narrowing as Internet use grows faster than any other medium, Americans are still more likely to read a newspaper or listen to news radio than to seek out news on the Web. At the same time, amateur journalists, so-called citizen journalists, are seeking to wrest control of news reporting from the professionals.

More and more traditional news outlets are incorporating citizen journalists as volunteer reporters and many—sometimes with the assistance of professionals—are running several Internet news sites.

The Knight Citizen News Network—supported by the journalism-oriented nonprofit Knight Foundation—offers training for citizen journalists and for those in traditional media who want to use the work of amateurs. It has identified about 800 citizen news media in the United States.

Americans are still more likely to read a newspaper or listen to news radio than to seek out news on the Web.

"They remain far from a substitute for legacy media," the PEJ report concluded, saying that the citizen sites' content tends to have less breadth, depth, quantity and quality than traditional media. Compared to mainstream news sites, the citizen sites tend not to be as timely, usually updated less than daily.

But average citizens are shaping the news in other ways, too, the report says. They're using search engines, such as Google, and aggregators, such as Google News, to locate stories of interest—often the work of professional journalists—and then sharing them via e-mail and social networking sites.

In addition, they're recommending news reports to others at sites designed for that purpose—Digg, Reddit and Topix, for example. They also recommend news items through Twitter, another social networking site that allows users to post messages of no more than 140 characters. Twitter has distinguished itself as a vehicle for on-site citizen reporting of fast-breaking news events, such as the recent Iran election protests and the terrorist attacks on Mumbai in November.

Most major traditional news media now incorporate links to news-sharing sites in stories and Web pages as a way to broaden reach. Some outlets also have accounts with social networks like Twitter and Facebook, and post links back to the stories on their own Web sites, as Miller-McCune.com does. During the 2008 campaign, YouTube provided a forum for sharing television news reports, campaign-produced videos and citizens' own products.

"By compiling, sharing and customizing the news they consume, people in a sense are becoming not only their own editors, but also critical agents in the trajectory of a news story," the PEJ report says.

In spite of the growth of citizen journalism, it still has few practitioners that produce original content. According to a Pew Center survey, just 4 percent of Americans have ever posted their own original news items, and just 7 percent have commented on news stories. Fifteen percent have signed up for e-mailed news alerts, nearly half have e-mailed a news story to a friend, and more than half use search engines to find news.

Traditional media (print, TV and radio) have reduced their reporting, staffs and product as a result of a huge downturn in advertising combined with a troubled economy. Internet advertising, particularly on the news sites, is nowhere near even old newspaper levels (or current levels, for that matter). As a result, a growing number of professional journalists, either by choice or by circumstance, are creating their own online news sites to fill some of the gaps.

These sites' missions range from covering local news to covering a niche topic with national or global scope. Some are nonprofits supported by philanthropy (such as Miller-McCune.com), some have fingers crossed that income can break even with expenses and eventually become profit-making businesses.

"Few if any are profitable or even self-sustaining," the report says. "For now, our sense is that they represent something complementary to the traditional news media. Yet something new is going on here that could grow beyond that."

Some notable examples:

MinnPost.com covers public affairs, arts, business and sports in Minnesota.

Arizonaguardian.com covers state government and politics for an audience willing to pay for a subscription.

Kaiser Health News Service, funded by the Kaiser Family Foundation covers health policy, publishes a Web site and makes its news available for free to other media.

GlobalPost.com retains a network of foreign correspondents on a part-time basis and publishes the work of freelancers.

ProPublica.org is a nonprofit investigative reporting organization that is supported by philanthropy. It makes its news available online and to other media for free, and conducts some investigations in partnership with other news organizations.

Politico.com, founded in 2007 with the goal of turning a profit, became a major source for national political news during the 2008 campaign and is now focusing on covering the federal government and national politics.

Traditional Media Still Dominant

Despite the traditional media's current financial and competitive difficulties, the report says, major news organizations that made their reputations in newspapers or television remain the dominant source for news on the Internet (such as *CNN* and the *New York Times*). Seven of the 10 most popular online news sites in 2008 were operated by some of those traditional media companies. Aggregators, such as *The Drudge Report*, *The Huffington Post* and various blogs, do little or no original reporting, instead linking to and commenting on traditional media's reports.

Newspapers, magazines, and radio and television news organizations are beefing up their online operations, and a 2007–08 survey by the University of Georgia's Cox Center for International Communication found a majority of newly hired journalists said their jobs included reporting for the Web.

Major news organizations that made their reputations in newspapers or television remain the dominant source for news on the Internet.

Journalists who work online are optimistic about the economic future of Internet news organizations, according to a survey sponsored by PEJ and the Online News Association, but they are concerned that journalistic standards are eroding online. They are worried especially that emphasis on speed is leading to careless reporting and a decline in accuracy.

Those survey results mesh with the report's authors' concern that round-the-clock cable news is pressuring journalists to make "minute-by-minute" judgments.

Traditional Media's Demise Could Be the End of Real News

Gary Kamiya

Gary Kamiya is cofounder of Salon, *an online news site.*

Journalism as we know it is in crisis. Daily newspapers are going out of business at an unprecedented rate, and the survivors are slashing their budgets. Thousands of reporters and editors have lost their jobs. No print publication is immune, including the mighty *New York Times*. As analyst Allan Mutter noted, 2008 was the worst year in history for newspaper publishers, with shares dropping a stunning 83 percent on average. Newspapers lost $64.5 billion in market value in 12 months.

All traditional media is in trouble, from magazines to network TV. But newspapers are the most threatened. For readers of a certain age, newspapers stand for a vanishing era, and the pleasures of holding newsprint in their hands is one that they are loath to give up. As a former newspaperman myself, like most of the original founders of *Salon*, I have a strong attachment to my dose of daily ink. I get most of my news online, but I still subscribe to both the local paper, in my case the *San Francisco Chronicle*, and to the *New York Times*. At parties and in casual conversations, speculation that newspapers might vanish like the dinosaurs that once ruled the earth spurs passionate jeremiads about the decline and fall of Western civilization.

But the real problem isn't that newspapers may be doomed. I would be severely disheartened if I was forced to

Gary Kamiya, "The Death of the News," *Salon*, February 17, 2009. This article first appeared in Salon.com, at http://www.Salon.com An online version remains in the Salon archives. Reprinted with permission.

abandon my morning ritual of sitting on my deck with a coffee and the papers, but I would no doubt get used to burning out my retinas over the screen an hour earlier than usual. As *Nation* columnist Eric Alterman recently argued, the real problem isn't the impending death of newspapers, but the impending death of *news*—at least news as we know it.

The real problem isn't the impending death of newspapers, but the impending death of news—at least news as we know it.

What is really threatened by the decline of newspapers and the related rise of online media is reporting—on-the-ground reporting by trained journalists who know the subject, have developed sources on all sides, strive for objectivity and are working with editors who check their facts, steer them in the right direction and are a further check against unwarranted assumptions, sloppy thinking and reporting, and conscious or unconscious bias.

If newspapers die, so does reporting. That's because the majority of reporting originates at newspapers. Online journalism is essentially parasitic. Like most TV news, it derives or follows up on stories that first appeared in print. Former *Los Angeles Times* editor John Carroll has estimated that 80 percent of all online news originates in print. As a longtime editor of an online journal who has taken part in hundreds of editorial meetings in which story ideas are generated from pieces that appeared in print, that figure strikes me as low.

There's no reason to believe this is going to change. Currently there is no business model that makes online reporting financially viable. From a business perspective, reporting is a loser. There are good financial reasons why the biggest content-driven Web business success story of the last few years, the Huffington Post, does very little original reporting. Reported pieces take a lot of time, cost a lot of money, require specialized skills and don't usually generate as much traffic as an Op-Ed screed, preferably by a celebrity. It takes a facile writer an hour to write an 800-word rant. Very seldom can the best daily reporters and editors produce copy that fast.

Currently there is no business model that makes online reporting financially viable. From a business perspective, reporting is a loser.

But the story is more complicated than that. At the same time that newspapers are dying, blogging and "unofficial" types of journalism continue to expand, grow more sophisticated and take over some (but not all) of the reportorial functions once performed by newspapers. New technologies provide an infinitely more robust feed of raw data to the public, along with the accompanying range of filtering, interpreting and commenting mechanisms that the Internet excels in generating.

As these developments expand, our knowledge of the world will become much less broad. Document-based reporting and academic-style research will increasingly replace face-to-face reporting. And the ideal of journalistic objectivity and fairness will increasingly crumble, to be replaced by more tendentious and opinionated reports.

The brave new media world will be one of tunnel vision and self-selected expertise, in which reported pieces are increasingly devoid of human interaction or human stories, often written by individuals who do not pretend to have a neutral stance. Raw, non-mediated video or audio will provide primary stories to anyone who is interested in them. In this imagined future, the New York Times will have died and only one or two wire services will still have reporters in, say, Gaza. In lieu of edited stories will be video interviews with Gaza inhabitants, as well as commentary and analysis from a vast army of experts, semi-experts and kibitzers. Consumers can set one info-dial to "Middle East primary feeds," set a commentary dial to "expert," "kibitzer" or "shuffle," set yet another to a targeted archival search of every academic paper written about Gaza. It will be feast and famine: There will be far less primary reporting done by professionals and far more information available to ordinary citizens.

This brave new info-world will have some advantages. So far, the Internet media revolution has been a huge net plus for journalism. It has greatly increased the quantity and quality of available opinion and (to a much lesser degree) news. Trying to figure out what the truth is about any given subject means reading about it from as many perspectives as possible, and exponentially more perspectives are accessible now. From foreign newspapers to brilliant bloggers, the Internet has given a voice to countless talented and informed people who would otherwise have no platform. It has empowered readers, created an army of bloggers who provide much-needed fact-checking and criticism of the entitled mandarins of the establishment press, and provided powerful counternarratives to the bland, centrist pablum so often served up by the "respectable" media.

All too often [the old media] has been sclerotic, incompetent and driven by hidden corporatist, nationalist or reactionary agendas.

Moreover, bloggers can also be valuable reporters, albeit ones who generally don't wear out much shoe leather. As *Slate* writer and media critic Jack Shafer has pointed out, some bloggers have done significant research reporting, digging through FOIA documents or unearthing official secrets.

As for the old media, it has not exactly always done a bang-up job of capturing reality. All too often it has been sclerotic, incompetent and driven by hidden corporatist, nationalist or reactionary agendas. The press's catastrophic failure to question the Bush administration's case for war in Iraq is the most glaring recent example, but there are many. "Professionalism" can be a vice, evidenced by the pathologically cozy relationship between many bigwig Beltway reporters and their government sources. Huffing and puffing about interloping amateurs all too often conceals the fact that those amateurs know as much or more about the subject as the professionals, and are not subject to being bamboozled by "insiders" with an agenda. Academic Middle East analysts, most of whom probably never picked up the phone in their life, but know the region's language and its history, were resoundingly right about the Iraq war. The professional journalism brigade, with its access to high-level sources and people on the ground, was disgracefully wrong. And the Internet has greatly empowered such academics.

The MSM's less than stellar record explains why in online forums and threads about this subject, many posters welcome the impending end of the media universe as we know it. But those who are calling for the demise of traditional media are throwing the baby out with the bath water—and the baby is reporting.

There is no substitute for field reporting, in which a real live human being observes an event while it is happening and talks to other real, live human beings. It is an immutable fact that firsthand observation is the building block not just of journalism, but of all human knowledge. This isn't just true in journalism, but in all fields, from science to the humanities. Academics acquire their knowledge through primary sources. Historians value firsthand accounts more than secondary ones, and give them more weight. The same is true for the law. An eyewitness to an event has more legal standing than someone who heard what the eyewitness said later.

If field reporting dies out, the world will become a less known place. Vast areas will simply not be covered, and those that are will not be covered from multiple perspectives. Precisely because reporters are imperfect, because they by necessity capture only a fragment of reality, it is essential that numerous firsthand accounts exist. If *Reuters*, the *Times* and all the other newspapers with foreign bureaus have died and only the *AP* reporter is telling us what happened in China, readers will be forced to accept his or her version without being able to compare it. And that faint gleam of empirical evidence will be lost amid the infinite amount of commentary that will instantly dominate the Internet.

> *There is no substitute for field reporting, in which a real live human being observes an event while it is happening and talks to other real, live human beings.*

The information universe today is not, of course, comprehensive, nor could it ever be. What appears in the newspapers is a result of editorial whim and financial pressures. But this limited and capricious hodgepodge of information is far preferable to the self-selected alternative that awaits us—it stimulates parts of our brain that would otherwise atrophy.

It's much easier to consume unfamiliar information in a newspaper than on the Internet. Because of the physical layout of a newspaper, you're much more likely to read a story you aren't interested in than you would if you were online. Even if the same reported stories were available online, they would not be as widely read. Online media is tailored to respond to the individual's conscious desires; it is less capable of stimulating latent ones.

A perfect example of why newspapers must continue to exist appeared in the *New York Times* on Feb. 1, 2009. Titled "Slain Exile Detailed Cruelty of the Ruler of Chechnya," the 3,700-word piece was reported from Vienna, London, Moscow, Oslo and Chechnya. It obviously took months of work and cost tens if not hundreds of thousands of dollars in salaries and expenses. And it revealed beyond any reasonable doubt that the president of Chechnya, Ramzan Kadyrov, is a murderous, sadistic thug who personally tortured many captured dissidents and ordered the assassination of a former insider who had fled to Vienna.

I would probably not have sought out this story on my own. But because it was on the front page of the *New York Times*, I read it. And as a result, my world expanded significantly.

If this kind of reporting dies out, the global consequences would be dire. Moral outrage would wither. Regimes would feel free to commit atrocities with impunity. As the Iraq and Gaza wars demonstrate, regimes prefer to wage controversial wars in the dark. Without reporting, dirty little wars would be invisible dirty little wars.

The civic consequences would be just as calamitous. With little empirical evidence about the world, the country would divide further into solipsistic, isolated communities. There would be no agreement on even the most rudimentary facts: We would look back nostalgically at those days when "only" half of Americans were so ill-informed, and susceptible to government propaganda, that they believed that Saddam Hussein was involved with 9/11. Rancorous division into exclusive camps would become even more pronounced than it is now, making political compromises even less likely. In this ignorant yet loudly opinionated future, our shared civic culture would degenerate, and demagogic leaders would flourish.

Karl Marx's prediction that capitalism would end up devouring itself has not stood up well (although there's a bit of leg-nibbling going on right now). But his dictum might end up being true for the news media.

The Internet gives readers what they want; newspapers give them what they need. And in a culture where the almighty market is always right, you can always get what you want—but you can't always get what you need. In their bottom-line desperation, newspapers are imitating the Internet. As Michael Hirschorn pointed out in a recent *Atlantic* article, papers are giving readers and advertisers what they think they want, blowing all their money on lifestyle and "consumer-friendly" pieces rather than on in-depth reporting.

Newspapers are institutions that adhere to a tradition of journalism and have the financial resources to carry on that tradition. Today, those institutions are threatened as never before.

If capitalism wins the battle, the result will be an unregulated marketplace of ideas in which consumers choose their own news—in effect, choose their own reality. Ironically, conservative devotees of the free market would find themselves living in a postmodern world right out of a seminar taught by Jacques Derrida. Nietzsche's credo that "there are no facts, only interpretations" will become our epistemological motto. In this deconstructed universe, not just readers, but the very idea of objective reality, would be the ultimate victim.

Historically, the only countervailing force against the market and the apotheosis of consumers' desires has been the institutional power of newspapers. Newspapers are institutions that adhere to a tradition of journalism and have the financial resources to carry on that tradition. Today, those institutions are threatened as never before, in part because of the disappearance of old-school publishers who regarded their media properties as a public trust, in part because of the rise of new media.

This bleak situation has given rise to a once-unthinkable notion: removing the news from market forces altogether by subsidizing it. In a recent Op-Ed in the *New York Times*, two business analysts suggested turning newspapers into "non-profit, endowed institutions—like colleges and universities."

Most journalists probably find something vaguely creepy about this idea; it's a little too high-minded, abstract and self-congratulatory to fit with their self-image as regular Joes and

Jills. There are also legitimate concerns whether foundations or other public supporters would influence editorial content or direction. But the alternative is disturbing.

A world without primary reporting will be literally less human. Talking to actual, live human beings, as opposed to reading documents or commentary or what they say online, has an innately moderating effect on one's approach. A good reporter sees issues in greater complexity because humans are complex. The Roman playwright Terence's credo "Nothing human is alien to me" is a noble one. But it will be harder to believe in it when actual human beings have vanished from the news. There is a reason why the online world, where humans are virtual, is prone to flame wars and creepy trolls. It is easier to despise someone you have never met. As writers who have worked online know, the simple act of replying courteously to a hostile poster usually leads them to become much more civil. And that is even truer of face-to-face interactions.

With all their flaws, traditional media institutions served as unifying forces in society. No one wants to go back to the days of network TV or the old *Time* magazine, when the media served as a quasi-official info-nanny telling citizens what to think. But a society without any shared sources of trusted information will be in danger of fragmenting. The old media acted as an institutional check on individual passions and prejudices. It served a Lockean function, upholding the social contract. The new world could be a Hobbesian one, a war of all against all.

Finally, the death of reporting will dangerously erode the ideal of objectivity. Newspapers embrace the institutional mission of objectivity: Their goal is to find out and report the truth about a given subject, no matter what that truth is. They are not supposed to go in looking for an answer, or holding preconceived beliefs. Of course, the distinction between fact and interpretation is only absolute in the simplest cases—it breaks down as soon as the event being covered acquires the least complexity or controversy. Reporters, like all human beings who are trying to make sense of complex experiences, must constantly make judgments that go beyond the mere facts. And the he-said, she-said approach mandated by objectivity can be ridiculously stupid. If Joe says the sky is blue and Jack, who is widely known to be a delusional psychotic who has just taken two tabs of acid, says it's purple with pink polka-dots, is it really necessary to report what Jack says?

But if perfect objectivity is impossible, that doesn't mean that it should not be the goal. The reporter's predisposition toward fact and fairness serves as a kind of ballast, a corrective to her natural instinct to make up her mind prematurely. And those who have not been trained and inculcated in an institution dedicated to objectivity are less likely to be able to do this. Institutions matter. And traditional journalistic institutions, newspapers in particular, are weighted toward fairness and objectivity. The Internet is not. Of course, bloggers or untrained writers are capable of being fair; indeed, the better bloggers are precisely those who fully and fairly engage with those who disagree with them. But the blogging ethos as a whole runs in the opposite direction. Being a reporter does not come naturally to bloggers.

The death of reporting will dangerously erode the ideal of objectivity.

No one can predict what the new information age will look like, and my version may be excessively dystopian. But one thing is indisputable: Reporting must be kept alive. With all its limitations and faults, it is a light that illuminates the world outside ourselves. And in an increasingly virtual and solipsistic age, that light is needed more than ever.

Organizations to Contact

The editors have compiled the following list of organizations concerned with the issues debated in this book. The descriptions are derived from materials provided by the organizations. All have publications or information available for interested readers. The list was compiled on the date of publication of the present volume; the information provided here may change. Be aware that many organizations take several weeks or longer to respond to inquiries, so allow as much time as possible.

The Century Foundation—Media and Politics
41 East 70th St., New York, NY 10021
(212) 535-4441 • fax: (212) 879-9197
website: http://tcf.org/politics

The Century Foundation is a nonprofit public policy research institution committed to the belief that a mix of effective government, open democracy, and competitive markets is the most effective solution to the major challenges facing the United States. The Foundation produces publications on various policies and issues, and one of its areas of interest is Media and Politics, which focuses on topics such as campaign finance reform, media criticism, polling analysis, and youth engagement with the goal of examining political life in the United States and advancing ideas for improving democracy. Recent commentaries in this topic area include "Social Media in This Age of Turmoil" and "The Future of News."

FactCheck.org
Annenberg Public Policy Center, 202 S. 36th St.
Philadelphia, PA 19104-3806
(215) 898-9400
e-mail: Editor@FactCheck.org
website: http://factcheck.org

FactCheck.org is a project of the Annenberg Public Policy Center of the University of Pennsylvania (APPC), a public policy research center. The FactCheck project acts as a nonpartisan, nonprofit watchdog that tries to reduce the level of deception and confusion in US politics by monitoring the factual accuracy of what is said by major political players in the form of TV ads, debates, speeches, interviews, and news releases. The project's website is a great source of articles examining recent public statements. It also offers Internet sources that provide impartial information and lesson plans to help students learn to analyze public policy issues. Recent articles include "Ryan's Budget Spin" and "Factchecking Obama's Budget Speech."

The Institute for the Study of the Judiciary, Politics, and the Media (IJPM)
Syracuse University College of Law, Syracuse, NY   13244
e-mail: kjbybee@maxwell.syr.edu
website: http://jpm.syr.edu/

Syracuse University's Institute for the Study of the Judiciary, Politics, and the Media (IJPM) is an academic institute devoted to the interdisciplinary study of issues at the intersection of law, politics, and the media. The institute sponsors lectures, conferences, and symposia designed to foster discussion and debate between legal scholars, sitting judges, and working journalists. IJPM also supports research and publishes publications relevant to the various intersections of law, politics, and the media. IJPM's e-journal, for example, includes articles such as "YouTube from Afghanistan to Zimbabwe: Tyrannize Locally, Censor Globally" and "Disclosure's Effects: Wikileaks and Transparency."

New Media Institute (NMI)
110 William St., 22nd Floor, New York, NY   10038
(917) 652-7141
website: www.newmedia.org

The New Media Institute (NMI) is a research and fact finding organization whose mission is to improve public understanding of issues surrounding the Internet and other forms new media communications. NMI works directly with the news media, researchers, academics, government and industry professionals and serves as a primary resource of facts, statistics, and analysis. The NMI website contains news, a law library, and commentaries on media issues. Examples of recent commentaries are: "Wikileaks—What Does This Mean for New Media?" and "Internet TV Survey—Revolution or Evolution?"

Pacific Research Institute (PRI)

One Embarcadero Center, Suite 350, San Francisco, CA 94111
(415) 989-0833 • fax: (415) 989-2411
website: www.pacificresearch.org

The Pacific Research Institute (PRI) is an organization committed to championing freedom, opportunity, and personal responsibility for all individuals by advancing free-market policy solutions. PRI provides the public with information on public policy issues through publications, events, media commentary, legislative testimony, and community outreach. A search of the PRI website for media and politics produces a number of articles, including "When Web 2.0 Meets Politics" and "Journalism, Citizen Politics and the Truth in the Era of Change."

Pew Research Center's Project for Excellence in Journalism

1615 L St. NW, Suite 700, Washington, DC 20036
(202) 419-3650 • fax: (202) 419-3699
e-mail: mail@journalism.org
website: www.journalism.org

The Pew Research Center's Project for Excellence in Journalism is a non-partisan, nonpolitical organization dedicated to trying to understand the information revolution using empirical methods to evaluate and study the performance of the press, particularly content analysis. The Project's goal is to help both the journalists who produce the news and the citizens who consume it develop a better understanding of what the press is delivering, how the media are changing, and what forces are shaping those changes. The Project produces an annual *State of the News Media* report that summarizes the trends in media, and its website is a source of commentaries, backgrounders, studies, and books on media issues.

ProPublica
One Exchange Plaza, 55 Broadway, 23rd Floor
New York, NY   10006
(212) 514-5250 • fax: (212) 785-2634
website: www.propublica.org

ProPublica is an independent, nonprofit newsroom that produces investigative journalism in the public interest. Its mission is to expose abuses of power and betrayals of the public trust by government, business, and other institutions at a time when many other news organizations are curbing this type of reporting. ProPublica hopes to carry on the great work of journalism in the public interest that is so important to democracy. The ProPublica website is a rich source of stories about various current events issues, including, for example, the dangers of gas drilling, the nuclear crisis in Japan, and the financial ties between doctors and medical companies.

United States Institute of Peace—Media, Conflict,
and Peacebuilding
2301 Constitution Ave. NW, Washington, DC   20037
(202) 457-1700 • fax: (202) 429-6063
website: www.usip.org/issue-areas/communications-and-media

The United States Institute of Peace is an independent, nonpartisan, national institution established and funded by Congress. Its goals are to help prevent and resolve violent international conflicts; promote post-conflict stability and development; and increase conflict management capacity, tools, and intellectual capital worldwide. The Institute does this by providing information, skills, and resources, as well as by directly engaging in peacebuilding efforts around the globe. The Institute's Media, Conflict, and Peacebuilding project focuses on the role media can play in peacebuilding and on countering the abuse of the media during conflicts. The website offers a long list of publications on this subject. Two recent examples are: *Social Media in the Middle East* and *Media and Peacebuilding: Trends in 2010 and Looking Ahead to 2011.*

Bibliography

Books

Megan Boler	*Digital Media and Democracy: Tactics in Hard Times.* Cambridge, MA: The MIT Press, 2010.
Jessica Clark and Tracy Van Slyke	*Beyond the Echo Chamber: Reshaping Politics Through Networked Progressive Media.* New York: New Press, 2010.
Alison Dagnes	*Politics on Demand: The Effects of 24-Hour News on American Politics.* New York: Praeger. 2010.
Wayne Errington and Narelle Miragliotta	*Media and Politics: An Introduction.* New York: Oxford University Press, 2007.
Doris A. Graber	*Media Power in Politics.* Washington, DC: CQ Press College, 2010.
Tauel Harper	*Democracy in the Age of New Media: The Politics of the Spectacle.* New York: Peter Lang Publishing, 2011.
Nadia Idle and Alex Nunns	*Tweets from Tahrir.* New York: OR Books, 2011.
Shanto Iyengar and Jennifer McGrady	*Media Politics: A Citizen's Guide.* New York: W.W. Norton, 2006.
Henry Jenkins	*Convergence Culture: Where Old and New Media Collide.* New York: NYU Press, 2008.

Yahya R. Kamalipour · *Media, Power, and Politics in the Digital Age: The 2009 Presidential Election Uprising in Iran.* Lanham, MD: Rowman & Littlefield, 2010.

Linda Jean Kenix · *Alternative and Mainstream Media: The Converging Spectrum.* London: Bloomsbury Academic, 2011.

Matthew Robert Kerbel · *Netroots: Online Progressives and the Transformation of American Politics.* Boulder, CO: Paradigm Publishers, 2009.

Bill Kovach and Tom Rosenstiel · *Blur: How to Know What's True in the Age of Information Overload.* New York: Bloomsbury USA, 2010.

Jeremy D. Mayer · *American Media Politics in Transition.* Columbus, OH: McGraw-Hill Humanities, 2007.

Robert W. McChesney and John Nichols · *The Death and Life of American Journalism: The Media Revolution That Will Begin the World Again.* New York: Nation Books, 2010.

Evgeny Morozov · *The Net Delusion: The Dark Side of Internet Freedom.* Washington, DC: PublicAffairs, 2011.

Philip Seib · *The Al Jazeera Effect: How the New Global Media Are Reshaping World Politics.* Dulles, VA: Potomac Books, 2008.

S. Craig Watkins   *The Young and the Digital: What the Migration to Social Network Sites, Games, and Anytime, Anywhere Media Means for Our Future.* Boston, MA: Beacon Press, 2010.

Periodicals and Internet Sources

Douglas Ahlers and John Hessen   "Traditional Media in the Digital Age," *Nieman Reports*, Fall 2005. www.nieman.harvard.edu.

Eric Alterman   "Think Again: What's Wrong with This Mainstream Media Picture?," Center for American Progress, July 29, 2010. www.americanprogress.org.

Douglas A. Blackmon and Sam Schechner   "Ads, Politics Blur Media Lines," *Wall Street Journal*, November 9, 2010. http://online.wsj.com.

Daniel Calingaert   "Making the Web Safe for Democracy," *Foreign Policy*, January 19, 2010. www.foreignpolicy.com.

John S. Carroll   "John S. Carroll on Why Newspapers Matter," *Nieman Watchdog*, April 28, 2006. www.niemanwatchdog.org.

James Chan   "Why Social Media Is a Dictator's Worst Nightmare," *Money Economics*, February 12, 2011. www.moneyeconomics.com.

Jason Easeley   "Conservative Media Bias: Bush Officials Outnumber Obama 6 to 1 On Sunday Shows," *PoliticusUSA*, May 7, 2011. www.politicususa.com.

Malcolm Gladwell "The Derivative Myth," gladwell.com, July 24, 2006. http://gladwell.typepad.com.

Malcolm Gladwell "Does Egypt Need Twitter?," *New Yorker*, February 2, 2011. www.newyorker.com.

Malcolm Gladwell and Clay Shirky "From Innovation to Revolution," *Foreign Affairs*, March/April 2011. www.foreignaffairs.com.

Ophaniel Gooding "Digital Era: Deleting the Dictators," *Awoko*, February 28, 2011. www.awoko.org.

Spencer Overton "The Shortcomings of Traditional Media in Covering Presidential Politics," techPresident, April 5, 2007. http://techpresident.com.

Samual F. Parent "Is Traditional Media Dead?," *Social Media Today*, April 3, 2010. http://socialmediatoday.com.

Tom Rosenstiel "Five Myths About the Future of Journalism," *Washington Post*, April 7, 2011. www.washingtonpost.com.

Doug Schoen "Newspapers Still Viable," *Huffington Post*, December 19, 2008. www.huffingtonpost.com.

Benjamin M. Scuderi "Maddow Discusses Politics and the Media," *Harvard Crimson*, November 15, 2010. www.thecrimson.com.

Kate Sheppard   "The Koch Brothers' Vast Right-Wing Media Conspiracy," *Mother Jones*, February 4, 2011. http://motherjones.com.

Clay Shirky   "The Political Power of Social Media," *Foreign Affairs*, January/February 2011. www.foreignaffairs.com.

Alan W. Silberberg   "Politics, Social Media, Beer and Guns," *Huffington Post*, April 21, 2010. www.huffingtonpost.com.

Linton Weeks   "Politics In the Social Media Age: How Tweet It Is," *NPR*, October 29, 2010. www.npr.org.

Michael Wolff   "Politico's Washington Coup," *Vanity Fair*, August 2009. www.vanityfair.com.

Daniel Young   "Does Fox Media Reflect a Trend for Traditional Media in the Future?," *Just Another 24 Hours*, October 6, 2010. http://justanother24hours.com.

Markos Moulitsas Zúniga   "FON: Traditional Media Navigates the Web Amid Bevy of Sources," *Abilene Reporter-News*, October 2, 2010. www.reporternews.com.

Markos Moulitsas Zúniga   "The Internet and Politics: Revolution.com," *Guardian*, January 4, 2010. www.guardian.co.uk.

Markos Moulitsas Zúniga   "'MSM' vs. 'Traditional Media,'" *Huffington Post*, August 15, 2007. www.huffingtonpost.com.

Index

O